THE BEST OF THE
BLACK HILLS

by ALAN LEFTRIDGE

FARCOUNTRY
PRESS

Spearfish Canyon, Chad Coppess, South Dakota Tourism

THE BEST OF THE
BLACK HILLS

by ALAN LEFTRIDGE

ACKNOWLEDGMENTS

My gratitude goes to the staff at Farcountry Press: Linda Netschert, Publisher; Kathy Springmeyer, Director of Publications; Will Harmon, Senior Editor; and Shirley Machonis, Senior Designer.

Special thanks go to Nancy Stimson, Choctaw, Chief of Interpretation and Education, Devils Tower National Monument; Bradley Block, Chief of Interpretation, Jewel Cave National Monument; and Riley Hays, Centennial Coordinator, Jewel Cave National Monument.

I especially wish to thank Linda, who shares my life, and who writes and edits along with me.

And lastly to acknowledge Marifran Wohlenberg, who, along with Linda, added to my appreciation of why everyone loves "the hills."

The completion of this book was possible because of the many people who provided information about, and expressed their passion for, the Black Hills. They are employees and volunteers of: Bear Butte State Park, Badlands National Park, Wind Cave National Park, Custer State Park, Mount Rushmore National Memorial, Adams Museum, The Journey Museum, Jewel Cave National Monument, Buffalo Gap National Grassland, and Black Hills National Forest.

ISBN: 978-1-56037-691-0

Cover photograph: Bison at Wind Cave National Park, Chad Coppess, South Dakota Tourism
Inset cover photographs: mountain bluebird, Neal Herbert, NPS; Mount Rushmore National Memorial, NPS photo, Rocky Mountain elk, Wind Cave National Park; blanket flower, Wind Cave National Park.

For more information about our books, write Farcountry Press, P.O. Box 5630, Helena, MT 59604; call (800) 821-3874; or visit www.farcountrypress.com.

Library of Congress Cataloging-in-Publication Data
Names: Leftridge, Alan, author.
Title: The best of the Black Hills / by Alan Leftridge.
Description: Helena, MT : Farcountry Press, 2017.
Identifiers: LCCN 2017034199 | ISBN 9781560376910 (pbk. : alk. paper)
Subjects: LCSH: Black Hills Region (S.D. and Wyo.)—Guidebooks.
Classification: LCC F657.B6 L44 2017 | DDC 917.83/904—dc23
LC record available at https://lccn.loc.gov/2017034199

 Produced and printed in the United States of America.

21 20 19 18 17   1 2 3 4 5

PREFACE

This is your first visit to the Black Hills, what should you see and do?
There is a lot. The Black Hills region is one of the best family vacation spots in the United States. Whether you are visiting one day or staying a week, you will discover an unparalleled number of activities to entertain and educate you and your loved ones.

The purpose of this book is to enhance your visit by sharing the natural history and cultural heritage of the Black Hills region as identified by some of the people who live here.

In a relatively small geographic area, the Black Hills region contains many iconic public sites, including two national parks, three national monuments, two national forests, two state parks, two state recreation areas, six scenic byways, several historic districts, two ghost towns, two national grasslands, and miles of open space.

Privately owned tourist attractions include the largest sculpted memorial in the country and the oldest tourist attraction in the Black Hills. A wide variety of concessionaires offer cave tours, horseback rides, jeep tours, amusement rides, zoos, mining tours, museums, fossil digs, zip lines, and summer stock theater performances.

This book focuses mostly on the resources offered by the public sector. They are the backbone of visitor activities. All of these places are featured in this book. The first three attractions on this list are must-visits. The ones that follow should be selected according to your travel itinerary and interests.

____ Mount Rushmore National Memorial
____ Crazy Horse Memorial
____ Deadwood Historic Site
____ Custer State Park
____ Needles Highway
____ Sylvan Lake
____ Legion Lake
____ Iron Mountain Road
____ Badlands National Park
____ Jewel Cave National Monument
____ Wind Cave National Park
____ Devils Tower National Monument
____ The Journey Museum
____ Rapid City Historic Business District

____ Spearfish Canyon Road
____ Bear Butte State Park
____ Buffalo Gap National Grassland

This book aims to inspire you to witness the rich natural and cultural heritage of the Black Hills. Follow your interests. Explore, hike, photograph, view wildlife and wildflowers, and learn about the people and events that make this place special. The experiences that you and your family have and the stories that you build will lead you to the spirit of the Black Hills.

—Alan Leftridge

Badlands National Park, Chad Coppess, South Dakota Tourism

HOW TO USE THE MAPS IN THIS BOOK

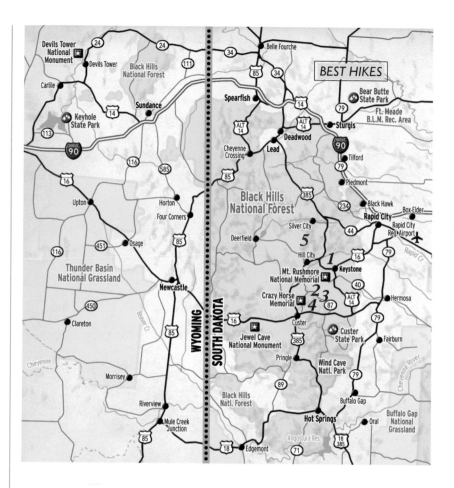

The maps in this book show numbered locations for sites and activities described in each chapter. Some indicate general areas, while others show more specific locations for individual subjects featured in the text. Use these maps with more detailed regional highway and visitor maps (such as the Black Hills National Forest map) to navigate the Black Hills. For hiking, mountain biking, skiing, horseback riding, or snowmobiling, even more detailed topographic maps are recommended, available at area sporting good stores.

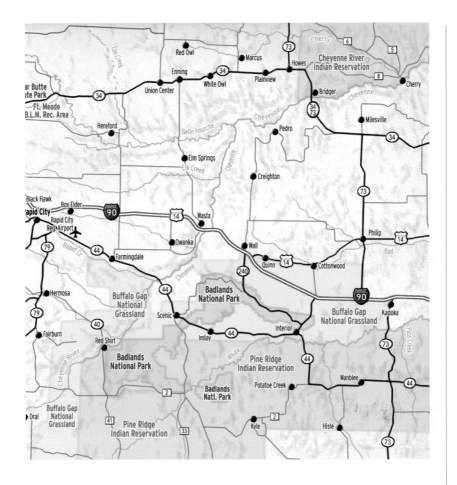

Bison, Chad Coppess, South Dakota Tourism

WHERE ARE THE BLACK HILLS?

Where prairie and forest meet, NPS photo

The Black Hills region inspires a sense of place. The essence of the Black Hills is in people's connections to its unique history, legends, and physical geography. Situated in western South Dakota and northeastern Wyoming, the Black Hills region is where the shortgrass prairie and tallgrass prairie overlap, forming a unique mixed-prairie environment. Projecting into the sky is a forested, mountainous island, the Black Hills. The entire region supports an array of plants and animals from the overlapping Rocky Mountains, Great Plains, and northern boreal ecosystems. Because of the region's lush environment, it is home to many indigenous animal species and over 1,500 plant types.

The area has attracted people for at least 10,000 years. Drawn to the region's wealth of resources, they found sustenance and spirituality in the rugged rock formations, canyons, grasslands, waterways, lakes, and caverns. The Black Hills are more than their tangible attributes. As you visit, you will sense why many generations have called this place home.

Why are the Black Hills not considered part of the Rocky Mountains? The reason is that they were formed differently. A dome of magma that pushed up and through layers of sedimentary rocks formed the Black Hills. The Rocky Mountains are a result of plate tectonics. Two huge continental blocks collided and one pushed skyward, creating the long sequence of mountain ranges that extends from Canada to Chile.

A BRIEF GEOLOGIC HISTORY OF THE BLACK HILLS

The basement of the Black Hills is made up of igneous rocks formed by repeated lava flows. Some of the volcanic layers were twisted and distorted underground as significant pressures transformed them into extremely hard metamorphic rocks.

On top of these igneous and metamorphic rocks, an ancient sea deposited sand, lime, and mud. The sea receded, leaving deposits that hardened into sedimentary sandstone, limestone, and shale.

A dome of molten rock lifted the basement rocks and some broke through the sedimentary layers. The resulting bulge formed the core of the Black Hills. You can see these ancient rocks around the town of Custer.

The outer edge of the core where the igneous and metamorphic rocks had not broken the surface were sandstone and shale. The sandstone was resistant to water and wind erosion; the shale eroded away. The sandstone landscape of steep ridges near Rapid City, Newcastle, and Sturgis are evidence of this process.

As the magma lifted the core, layers of shale near the edges eroded, leaving a valley that encircles the entire Black Hills known as "the Race Track." The town of Hot Springs is in this valley.

Other rock layers were eroding, too. Endless cycles of annual rainfall molded limestone into fantastic rock formations around the margins of the Black Hills. Millions of years of groundwater migration dissolved limestone layers and formed all of the caves in the region.

All of these processes continue. Geologically, the Black Hills are young.

Needles, Beth Steinhauer, Black Hills National Forest

BEST NAMES OF NATURAL FEATURES

Mount Rushmore National Memorial, NPS photo

Many of the features in the Black Hills bear interesting or lyrical names. Here are some that pique visitors' curiosity the most.

Black Elk Peak

Until August 12, 2016, this 7,242-foot peak was Harney Peak, named for U.S. Army General William Harney, who fought against Native Americans during the Plains Indian War. Today, its name honors Black Elk, second cousin of Crazy Horse and revered Oglala Lakota medicine man.

Devils Tower

According to Colonel Richard Dodge, the Native Americans called it "the bad god's tower." In his book *The Black Hills*, published in 1876, Dodge named it Devils Tower.

Needles Eye

The identity of the person who named this peculiarly shaped rock along the Needles Highway near Sylvan Lake is lost to antiquity. Its resemblance to the eye of a sewing needle is easy to recognize.

Deadwood

An early gold seeker referred to the area as deadwood for the burned and dying trees lining the gulch. The name stuck.

Bear Butte

The Lakota people referred to the geologic feature as *Mato Paha* or Bear Mountain. Anglo-Europeans, in turn, called it Bear Butte. It is technically an igneous intrusion like Devils Tower.

Mount Rushmore National Memorial

It is named for Charles Rushmore, a New York attorney who specialized in mining law. He made several trips to the Black Hills in the 1880s.

Needles Eye, Alan Leftridge

BLACK HILLS: JUST THE FACTS

- The Black Hills is an English translation of the Lakota name, *Paha Sapa*, which translates to "hills that are black." Although the ponderosa pine forests are green, they appear black from a distance.

- The Black Hills region is in western South Dakota and northeastern Wyoming, comprising an area 125 miles long and 65 miles wide, about the size of New Jersey.

- The highest point in South Dakota east of the Rocky Mountains is Black Elk Peak at 7,242 feet. It is also the tallest mountain between the Rocky Mountains and Europe.

- Most rocks of the Badlands are too young to hold dinosaur fossils, but fossil mammals are superbly represented here.

- Devils Tower is the first national monument. President Theodore Roosevelt signed the executive order establishing the monument in 1906.

- Evans Plunge in Hot Springs is the oldest tourist attraction in the Black Hills, operating since 1890.

- At 71,000 acres, Custer State Park is the largest state park in South Dakota. It is also the oldest.

- Custer is the oldest town in the Black Hills. It was named after Lt. Col. George Armstrong Custer, who led an expedition through the region in 1874, two years before his demise at the Battle of the Little Bighorn.

A BRIEF CULTURAL HISTORY OF THE BLACK HILLS

Lakota camp, John C. H. Grabill,
Library of Congress LC-DIG-ppmsc-02507

The Black Hills region is rich in Native American and early settler history. Archaeological evidence suggests that human use of the area began about 10,000 years ago. People roamed freely on the land until France laid claim to the region in the late 1670s. France passed the area off to Spain in 1762, which returned it to France in 1800. The United States acquired the Black Hills as part of the Louisiana Purchase in 1802. By then, the Lakota people were in permanent residence throughout western South Dakota. Euro-American settlements did not exist, though adventurers, explorers, and trappers roamed the area.

Growing conflicts among the various Native American tribes and clashes with encroaching settlers caused the government to intervene. The 1868 Fort Laramie Treaty created a Lakota reservation that included the Black Hills, and it prohibited immigrant settlement without prior approval from the Lakota.

The first official government expedition to explore the Black Hills was Lt. Col. George Armstrong Custer's 1874 incursion. Among the 1,000 expedition members were two miners who found gold in French Gulch. Word spread. Throngs of fortune hunters violated the treaty by setting up gold camps. Violence ensued between the miners and Native Americans. The U.S. government stepped in, seized the Great Sioux Reservation in 1877, broke it into several smaller reservations, and then allowed settlement. Most of the towns in the Black Hills were established at this time, all near gold strikes.

The Deadwood Coach, circa 1889, John C. H. Grabill, Library of Congress LC-DIG-ppmsc-02600

This period in Black Hills history brought a convergence of several "larger than life" personalities. Many of these people became legendary characters—George A. Custer, Calamity Jane, Crazy Horse, Standing Bear, Sitting Bull, General George Crook, Seth Bullock, Wild Bill Hickok, and Buffalo Bill Cody—and helped define a Western mythology.

The days of lawlessness waned by the mid-1880s, and large corporations began to dominate gold and silver mining. The economy stabilized over the next two decades, but the region's economy needed more industry to continue growing. Politician Peter Norbeck envisioned the Black Hills as a potential tourist mecca. State historian Doane Robinson recommended to Norbeck that a grand patriotic monument would draw generations of tourists. He was correct. Tourism is among the top industries today in the Black Hills.

A land that was home to nomadic people for thousands of years, once declared a possession by the Spanish and French, is today one of the greatest vacation draws in the United States.

CIVILIAN CONSERVATION CORPS IN THE BLACK HILLS

CCC workers at Wind Cave NP, NPS photo

When President Franklin D. Roosevelt took office in 1933, the United States was in a deep economic depression. To help vitalize the economy, the president envisioned and Congress established the Civilian Conservation Corps (CCC). The purpose of the CCC was to put thousands of unemployed men to work on public lands. The assignments were administered out of military-style camps from which young men carried out multiple conservation and construction projects.

The Black Hills had twenty-six CCC camps. For the next nine years, corps members completed hundreds of projects throughout the region. The CCC honored South Dakota's Senator Peter Norbeck's directive that all tasks were to complement the Black Hills' primitive charm. Among the jobs that the CCC completed were numerous stone and log bridges, several campgrounds, miles of trails, dozens of picnic areas and shelters, road construction and improvement projects, many miles of roadway stone retaining walls, laying underground telephone lines, forest improvement projects, and wildlife rehabilitation.

Many of the assignments that corps members completed are still in use. As you tour the Black Hills look for these: the Black Hills Playhouse (an intact example of a CCC camp); Wildlife Station Visitor Center; "pigtail bridges" of Iron Mountain Road; Custer State Park Museum; Mount Coolidge Fire Lookout; Black Elk (Harney) Peak Fire Tower; the dams that formed Legion, Stockade, Center, and Horsethief Lakes; fish hatchery ponds in Rapid City; several administrative buildings in Wind Cave National Park; and most of the buildings, roads, and trails in Devils Tower National Monument.

The rustic designs in wood and stone are distinctive. As you tour the Black Hills, see if you can identify structures built by those men who President Roosevelt liked to refer to as his "tree army."

NOTABLE PEOPLE OF THE BLACK HILLS

Few places are as rich in legend and lore as the Black Hills. Knowing about some of the people who contributed to the character of the area will enrich your holiday. While touring the region, you will see the names of many people whose actions and personalities define the essence of the area. You will see the names of great Native American leaders such as Crazy Horse, Henry Standing Bear, and Sitting Bull; military officers like George Armstrong Custer and George Crook; civic leaders, for example, Sol Star and Seth Bullock; gamblers like Wild Bill Hickok and Poker Alice; monument builders, namely, Gutzon Borglum, Korczak Ziolkowski, and Peter Norbeck; and characters the likes of Calamity Jane and Potato Creek Johnny. This section gives you a brief overview of how some of these people influenced the Black Hills, making the region what it is today.

Crazy Horse (1842–1877)

You may see a representative likeness of Crazy Horse, but no authenticated photograph exists. He refused to have his image taken for various personal and spiritual reasons, stating to Dr. Valentine T. McGillycuddy, "My friend, why should you wish to shorten my life by taking from me my shadow?" No one today knows what he looked like, but a gigantic monument is being sculpted of him to honor all Native American heroes.

Crazy Horse is an excellent choice for a statue. He was a notable and iconic Plains Indian. Like many Native Americans, he resisted yielding to the norms of the encroaching settlers, saying, "One does not sell the earth upon which the people walk." As a Lakota leader, he was committed to saving his people's cultural heritage.

Born near Bear Butte, he is described to have been near average in height, lithe in build, with a light complexion and curly hair. His name was Tashunka Witko, literally "His-Horse-Is-Crazy," shortened to Crazy Horse, and it may have been passed to him from his father with the same name.

Life for Crazy Horse and the Lakota people began to change in the 1850s as settlers migrated into tribal territory. Competition for resources brought cultural clashes. Army forts were built on the Great Plains to protect the settlers and to force all Native American tribes onto reservations. Crazy Horse, Sitting Bull, Gall, and other great leaders resisted. Conflicts intensified between the tribes and the United States, leading to the Plains Indian War. Crazy Horse was central to many of the battles that followed, including the Fetterman Massacre, the Battle of the Rosebud, and the Battle of the Little Bighorn.

After Custer's defeat at the Little Bighorn River, the U.S. Army pursued Crazy Horse and his people throughout the winter. The band grew weary from being hunted, and himself exhausted, Crazy Horse surrendered to federal troops in May 1877. The army officially arrested him on September 5, concerned that he might flee confinement. He was killed during a scuffle with his captors while being escorted to a guardhouse.

Crazy Horse endeavored to uphold his people's customs. But he also was a visionary who said, "Treat the earth well: it was not given to you by your parents, it was loaned to you by your children."

George A. Custer, Library of Congress, LC-DIG-ppmsca-33129

George Armstrong Custer (1839–1876)

You may know of George Armstrong Custer for his "Last Stand" at the Battle of the Little Bighorn, June 25, 1876. It was there that he chose to lead five companies of the 7th Cavalry in an attack on a miles-long Native American encampment along what the natives called the Greasy Grass River. Custer's orders were to force them onto reservations. He miscalculated the response of the Indians. Hundreds of Lakota and Cheyenne warriors surged from their village on horseback and pursued the five companies across the rolling landscape, killing Custer and annihilating those under his command, including two of his brothers, a nephew, and a brother-in-law.

Custer considered himself a military commander, a plainsman, and a pathfinder. Two years before the Battle of the Little Bighorn, he persuaded his superiors to allow him to lead an expedition into the Black Hills. Even today people speculate and debate the purpose and legality of that army incursion into tribal lands.

Custer's 1874 expedition of 1,000 troopers traveled for almost two weeks across the summer prairie until reaching the Black Hills region. They found the area abounding in wildflowers, so prolific and tall that the plants tickled the bellies of the soldiers' steeds. For the next five weeks, they explored the Black Hills, cutting roads, climbing peaks, hunting game, and enjoying the scenery as visitors do today. Some detractors in the press corps referred to the expedition as a picnic.

The assemblage included two well-seasoned prospectors who searched for evidence that the Black Hills contained gold. They found some indications, but not El Dorado. Rich lodes were later discovered by fortune seekers who stampeded to the region, lured by Custer's official report.

Custer's name and fame are indelibly etched on the area through lore and in noticeable ways. As you tour the Black Hills country, you will find a forest, a town, and a state park bearing his name. How many more times can you count the name of Custer on your travels?

James Butler "Wild Bill" Hickok (1837–1876)

James Butler "Wild Bill" Hickok, George G. Rockwood photo

When those who began to eulogize the myth of the West sought a single figure to symbolize the lawman as hero, they found Wild Bill Hickok an ideal character. He had all the attributes of a Wild West lawman: courage, distinguished looks, a marksman's eye, calm demeanor, and total confidence in himself.

Most of Hickok's life was spent in Missouri, Kansas, Nebraska, and Texas where he was a frontiersman, farmer, Union Army spy, cavalry scout, stagecoach driver, canal boat pilot, wagon master, and farmer. Later in life he even tried showmanship. For a brief time, he worked for the U.S. Army hunting horse thieves and became close friends with George Armstrong Custer.

Custer's wife, Libbie, described Hickok as "a delight to look upon. Tall, lithe, and free in every motion, he rode and walked as if every muscle was perfection . . . [the] frank, manly expression of his fearless eyes and his courteous manner gave one a feeling of confidence in his word and in his undaunted courage."

He is best remembered in truth and lore as a lawman and a gunfighter. His accomplishments as a lawman are well documented. He served in Kansas as sheriff in Hays City and marshal of Abilene. Both towns were rough places filled with dangerous individuals. History differs on the number of people he killed. Hickok once claimed over 100. Some say he may have killed as many as thirty-six. Other historians have a more conservative number of fewer than ten. Regardless of the truth, his perceived deeds made him a legend in his own time.

Hickok's gunfighting and peacekeeping days ended in 1871 when he was involved in a melee that resulted in him accidently killing his deputy. The town relieved him of his duties. The killing haunted him to the point of never engaging in another gun battle.

Sometimes arrested as a vagrant, he began living off of his reputation, gambling, and even appearing in Buffalo Cody's Wild West Show. In March 1876, he left his honeymoon with Agnes Lake, a circus performer eleven years his senior, and headed for the Black Hills' goldfields. He hoped to make a "strike" and bring Agnes out West. Catching Charlie Utter's wagon train in Cheyenne, he arrived in Deadwood in mid-July.

Hickok's wild exploits came to an end when he was thirty-nine years old while playing cards in Nuttal & Mann's Number 10 Saloon. Ironically, the most celebrated lawman and folk character in the West was murdered with both his pistols in their holsters. He did not see his assailant coming and was killed instantly. The cards that Hickok had been dealt were a pair of black aces and a pair of black eights, with the fifth card the jack of diamonds. This would be forever known as "the dead man's hand."

Jack McCall, public domain

John "Jack" McCall (1850–1877)

Many people wished Wild Bill Hickok harm, and some had long-standing grudges. But Jack McCall acted on his grievance impetuously. An emotionally disturbed vagrant, he traveled about, seeking the excitement of gold camps. On August 1, 1876, in a card game with Hickok, McCall lost everything and was humiliated when Wild Bill offered him some money to get by. The next day, McCall returned to Nuttal & Mann's Number 10 Saloon and saw Hickok sitting at a poker table with his back turned. McCall stepped forward and shot Hickok in the head, killing him instantly.

McCall stood trial for murder in Deadwood two days later. He was acquitted because he declared that he killed Hickok in retribution for killing his brother, and also because the town leaders knew that the trial had no legal standing.

Fearing danger, McCall left Deadwood for Laramie, where he boasted about killing Hickok. What he did not understand was that the Black Hills and Deadwood were on Indian land, where the U.S. government had no jurisdiction. Now, back in U.S. territory, McCall was arrested and taken to Yankton, the capital of the Dakota Territory, for trial. In December 1876, he was found guilty of murder and sentenced to hang.

On March 1, 1877, Jack McCall was the first person to be executed in Dakota Territory, and nearly every able-bodied person in the capital witnessed the event. When asked why he shot Wild Bill in the back of his head, McCall declared that it would have been suicide to face him.

Charlie Utter (1838–1912?)

Best known as a close friend of Wild Bill Hickok, "Colorado" Charlie Utter was one of the characters who fed the mythology of Deadwood. Standing at five feet, six inches, Charlie presented a striking appearance. His hair was long and blond, his mustache the same.

Charlie Utter (kneeling) and Steve at Wild Bill Hickok's grave, public domain

Scribner's Monthly magazine described him thusly: "Dressed in his trapper-suit, Charley presents a figure well worth looking at. Buckskin coat and pantaloons . . . vest of buckskin tanned with the hair on, and clasped with immense bear-claws instead of buttons; pistol, knife, and tomahawk in belt, the belt-buckle of Colorado silver and very large; a broad-brimmed hat and stout moccasins—these are the externals of this famous Rocky mountain guide."

Born in Illinois, Charlie moved to Colorado by the 1860s and earned a reputation as a trapper, prospector, and mountain guide. When gold was found in the Black Hills, he organized a wagon train to the gold-fields in the spring of 1876.

Adventurers, prospectors, entrepreneurs, and ne'er-do-wells gathered in communities along possible routes to get safe passage into the Indian lands. Wild Bill joined the wagon train when it arrived in Cheyenne. Calamity Jane hitched on to the party at Fort Laramie. Together, they arrived in Deadwood in July 1876. Utter started an express delivery service to Cheyenne and immediately prospered.

Utter and Wild Bill likely knew each other from their days in Kansas and Colorado. Utter considered himself Wild Bill's unofficial protector, safeguarding him from his excessive drinking and gambling self.

When Wild Bill was murdered days after arriving in Deadwood, Charlie claimed his body and paid for the funeral expenses and burial plot. The wooden grave marker read in part:

Pard, we will meet again in the Happy
Hunting Ground. To part no more, Goodbye.
Colorado Charlie, C. H. Utter

Three years later he helped rebury Wild Bill in Mount Moriah Cemetery.

Charlie Utter left the Black Hills by 1880, moving to New Mexico and later Panama, where he practiced as a druggist and physician. When he was last seen at his pharmacy in 1910, he was blind and grizzled. When and where he died are unknown.

Calamity Jane, H. R. Locke,
Library of Congress, LC-DIG-ds-05297

Martha "Calamity Jane" Canary (1856–1903)

Calamity Jane's name is rooted in legend and tied forever to the Black Hills. No other woman in the American West has more fictionalized stories attributed to her.

Born Martha Jane Canary in Missouri, her family relocated to Virginia City during Montana's gold rush. Adventure attracted her. She took a variety of jobs including mule skinner, bullwhacker, railroad employee, dancehall girl, and cook.

Her rowdy lifestyle, public drunkenness, and tall tales gained attention. She donned buckskins for pictures and promotional appearances but normally wore dresses. Contrary to the myriad stories about her, there is no historical record that she arrested outlaws, robbed banks, cured the sick, or killed any people.

One description of her from the early 1870s by John Hunton was that "her achievements have been greatly magnified by every writer I have ever met, for she was among the commonest of her class."

In July 1876, Calamity Jane's attention turned toward unruly Deadwood. She joined Charlie Utter's wagon train as it passed through Fort Laramie. Wild Bill Hickok, who was traveling from Cincinnati to Deadwood, was among those on the journey. It is said that this is when the two became acquainted. Speculations about the depth of their relationship are part of her legend. She delightfully fed people stories, including that she and Wild Bill were sweethearts and had a child. In truth they knew each other for only about three weeks before he was killed.

Her life of excess did not need exaggerating. A rambunctious lifestyle, fueled by chronic alcoholism, led to many ailments that contributed to her death in Terry, South Dakota, at the age of fifty-one. Securing her legacy with Wild Bill, she requested that she be buried next to him in Deadwood's Mount Moriah Cemetery.

Sol Star (1840–1917)

Solomon Star was a respected and beloved public servant, politician, and entrepreneur who helped bring civility and prosperity to Deadwood.

Born in Bavaria in 1840, he was ten years old when his parents sent him to live with his uncle in Ohio. After finishing school and working in his uncle's garment business, he struck out for adventure in Montana. It was in Helena where he met and became a lifelong friend of Seth Bullock. The partners started a hardware store there and then moved their business to Deadwood in 1876.

Sol Star, Deadwood History

Star quickly became a celebrated and respected leader in the Deadwood community. First as a business owner, then as its mayor for five terms. Today, Sol Star would be considered a social activist. He was a central figure in Deadwood's Jewish community, and he worked to win the trust of the Chinese residents at a time when whites viewed them as second-class citizens.

He never married and lived alone at his ranch until his death in 1917. His funeral was the biggest and grandest ever held in Deadwood. You will not find his grave in Mount Moriah Cemetery; he is buried in St. Louis.

Seth Bullock, Theodore Roosevelt Center, Dickinson State University

Seth Bullock (1849–1919)

A Deadwood legend, Seth Bullock presented the image of a quintessential Western lawman. Tall and imposing with an aquiline nose and stern eyes, "he could outstare a mad cobra or a rogue elephant," declared a grandson.

Born in Ontario, Canada, Seth ran away from home at sixteen years old to be with his sister in Montana; she sent him back. He was excited about the American West and returned to Helena, Montana, when he was twenty. Bullock took up auctioneering and found a business partner there named Sol Star. Bullock ran for office and was elected to the Territorial Senate and as sheriff of Lewis and Clark County.

Seeing a good business opportunity in upstart Deadwood, Star and Bullock packed wagons with hardware goods and arrived there August 1, 1876, the day before Jack McCall murdered Wild Bill.

They sold supplies out of a tent, and later from their hardware store. Bullock soon became a leading figure, and with the escalating violence in Deadwood, sought the governor's appointment as sheriff of Lawrence County.

Bullock was bringing a horse thief into Deadwood when a life-changing moment occurred. He happened upon Teddy Roosevelt near present-day Belle Fourche. Roosevelt was a deputy sheriff in Medora, North Dakota. The strangers shared stories and began a friendship. Roosevelt claimed that "Seth Bullock is a true westerner, the finest type of frontiersman." So close was their bond that Bullock volunteered as one of Roosevelt's Rough Riders during the Spanish-American War. He didn't see action but acquired the nickname "Captain."

Bullock campaigned for Roosevelt's presidency and attended his 1905 inauguration. The *Chicago Tribune* noted that Bullock "attracted general attention around the White House today. He has a fierce looking melodrama-villain's mustache and wears a sombrero."

Bullock grieved over Roosevelt's death in 1919. He erected a memorial to the president on Mount Roosevelt with the help of the Society of Black Hills Pioneers. Bullock died several months later of colon cancer and is buried above Mount Moriah Cemetery where his grave site looks toward the Roosevelt Monument, across Deadwood Gulch.

Poker Alice (1851–1930)

Poker Alice, South Dakota State Historical Society

Poker Alice is a Black Hills legend. Born in Devonshire, England, her maiden name was Ivers. She eventually had three married surnames: Duffield, Tubbs, and Huckert. Mr. Duffield, a mining engineer in Leadville, Colorado, taught her how to play faro and poker. After he died in a mining accident, she became an adept gambler, traveling throughout the West. Her playing prowess and attractiveness drew men to her poker table. With a cigar in her mouth and pistol at the ready, she often won more than $6,000 nightly. She relished telling her rivals, "Praise the Lord and place your bets. I'll take your money with no regrets."

She arrived in the Black Hills about 1903 and soon married Warren Tubbs. Following his early death from tuberculosis, she moved to the Fort Meade area near Bear Butte and opened a brothel, continuing to deal poker. One night in 1913, she attempted to quell several unruly soldiers with a rifle shot. The bullet ripped into two soldiers, killing one. She was found innocent of murder, but the authorities closed her brothel. Alice moved to Sturgis about 1919, becoming a speakeasy owner and whiskey bootlegger during Prohibition. Later, she returned to her familiar career and opened another brothel near Fort Meade. Afflicted with a painful gall bladder, she was forced to retire to a small nearby cottage.

Favored photographs of Alice are as a gruff-looking, cigar-chewing seventy-year-old. For most of her life, she was considered attractive, wearing only the finest clothes. She died from complications of a gall bladder operation at seventy-nine years of age.

John "Potato Creek Johnny" Perrett (1866–1943)

A great many colorful characters have lived in Deadwood. Few are more of a caricature of a time and place than John Perrett, aka "Potato Creek Johnny."

The four-foot, three-inch Perrett immigrated to the United States from Wales in 1883 when he was seventeen years old. He made his way

Potato Creek Johnny, Deadwood History

to the Black Hills, well after the initial gold rush of the 1870s. John worked several jobs for the next eight years and then resolved to try gold prospecting, staking a claim on Potato Creek.

For thirty-eight years, John made a living working his claim, all the while assuming an eccentric appearance. He savored looking the part of a crusty old prospector. He wore archetypical prospector clothes and grew his hair long, with a beard to match.

Then, almost fifty years after the 1870s gold rush, Johnny made a find that crystallized his fame. He found in his pan the largest nugget ever seen in the Black Hills. Some people asserted that the leg-shaped stone, which weighs 7.346 troy ounces (about half a pound), is several nuggets fused together. Nonetheless, Johnny became an instant Deadwood legend. To the delight of tourists, he cultivated the iconic caricature of a crusty prospector, spinning yarns and acting the part.

A likeness of the nugget is often on exhibit at the Adams Museum in Deadwood. The real nugget was purchased by Deadwood businessman William E. Adams for $250 and is today secured in a vault.

John Perrett is buried in Mount Moriah Cemetery alongside such characters as Calamity Jane and Wild Bill Hickok.

Peter Norbeck (1870–1936)

Peter Norbeck believed that he could transform the landscape into works of art for tourism. As South Dakota's governor, he championed the construction of the Needles Highway, personally laying out most of its route. Then, as a senator, he wrote to South Dakota's new governor, Carl Gunderson, about the idea of a Mount Rushmore monument, stating, "I think this might be an opportunity to secure one of the national attractions in this country of

Peter Norbeck, Bain News Service, Library of Congress, LC-DIG-ggbain-21896

the highest artistic quality." Gunderson agreed, and Senator Norbeck began working to secure government funding for the monument.

While workers carved Mount Rushmore, Norbeck encouraged the construction of the Iron Mountain Road, plotting much of its route as he had the Needles Highway. Viewpoints that framed Mount Rushmore were of special interest to Norbeck.

Iron Mountain Road and the Needles Highway were meant to interplay with nature and highlight the beauty of the Black Hills. Peter Norbeck influenced visitor experiences in the Black Hills, including pushing for development around Sylvan Lake and securing the designations of Badlands National Park, Custer State Park, and Wind Cave National Park.

Peter Norbeck's legacy to the Black Hills is enduring. Millions of visitors, like yourself, are introduced to the natural beauty of the Black Hills through his aesthetic vision. "I would rather be remembered as an artist," he said, "than as a United States senator." In honor of his contributions to visitor experiences, you will find several features named for him, including Norbeck Scenic Byway, Norbeck Visitor Center, and Norbeck Overlook.

Gutzon Borglum (1867–1941)

Born in 1867 near Bear Lake, Idaho, John Gutzon de la Mothe Borglum showed a talent for art at a young age. He later studied sculpture in Paris where he befriended Auguste Rodin and became influenced by his light-catching style. Returning to the United States, Borglum embarked on a career as a sculptor. His bust of Abraham Lincoln, carved from a six-ton block of marble, sits today in the Crypt of the U.S. Capitol.

Gutzon Borglum, Harris & Ewing, Library of Congress, LC-DIG-hec-19092

Gutzon focused on interpreting patriotic images and memorializing American achievement. The United Daughters of the Confederacy commissioned him to carve a memorial frieze of leaders of the Confederacy on Stone Mountain, near Atlanta, Georgia. He unveiled the head of Robert E. Lee in 1924 but soon became embroiled in a dispute with his benefactors and left the project after smashing his plaster models. The sheer scale of the Stone Mountain work provided great challenges and lessons, however, preparing Borglum for the massive undertaking that would occupy the remainder of his life.

South Dakota state historian Doane Robinson was aware of Borglum's work on Stone Mountain. Robinson recommended to Senator Peter Norbeck that Gutzon could carve a patriotic tourist attraction in the Black Hills. Originally conceived to be several pillars of famous people among the Needles, Borglum convinced them to switch to a grander project, the carving of Mount Rushmore. "The purpose of the memorial," Borglum said, "is to communicate the founding, expansion, preservation, and unification of the United States with colossal statues of Washington, Jefferson, Lincoln, and Theodore Roosevelt." Work began in 1927 with funds raised by South Dakota Governor Carl Gunderson.

Borglum did not live to see the completion of Mount Rushmore; he died in March 1941. His son, Lincoln, became the first superintendent of the monument and continued sculpting the mountain. Work on the monument officially stopped October 31, 1941, leaving it as you see it today, unfinished.

Chief Henry Standing Bear (1874–1953)

"My fellow chiefs and I would like the white man to know that the red man had great heroes too." Those words were penned by Chief Henry Standing Bear, who initiated and pursued the idea of a monument to a great Native American leader.

Standing Bear was born a Brule Lakota, near Pierre, South Dakota, at a time of great change in the American West. A cousin of Crazy Horse, Standing Bear was educated at the Carlisle Indian Industrial School in Pennsylvania. There he was given the name Henry, and he learned the ways of the white world. He developed leadership and communication skills that prepared him to be a leader of his Lakota people.

Chief Standing Bear wanted a memorial of Crazy Horse, and he lobbied Gutzon Borglum to include a likeness of Crazy Horse on Mount Rushmore along with the presidents. He was rebuffed. Standing Bear turned to sculptor Korczak Ziolkowski, who finally accepted after ten years of persistent persuasion. Standing Bear declared that the memorial "is to be entirely an Indian project under my direction." Ziolkowski agreed, and he began work on the Crazy Horse Memorial in 1947.

Today, more than 1 million people annually visit the Crazy Horse

Memorial project. Look for photographs and information about Chief Henry Standing Bear when you visit the visitor center. If it were not for his leadership and perseverance, the carving honoring all American Indian leaders would have never begun.

Korczak Ziolkowski (1908–1982)

"When your life is over, the world will ask you only one question: 'Did you do what you were supposed to do?'"
—Korczak Ziolkowski

A Bostonian of Polish ancestry, Korczak Ziolkowski (pronounced COR-chalk jewel-CUFF-ski) was an acclaimed sculptor who devoted the second half of his

Korczak Ziolkowski, Deadwood History

life to carving the Crazy Horse Memorial in the Black Hills. The project was (and still is) a mammoth undertaking that only an experienced carver could attempt.

Ziolkowski learned how to use heavy construction equipment from his foster father and began wood carving at an early age. While in his twenties, he turned to sculpting marble, which brought him acclaim throughout New England. At the 1939 New York World's Fair, Ziolkowski won first prize for his marble statue of Polish pianist and politician Ignacy Paderewski. Gutzon Borglum hired Korczak that same year to assist on the Mount Rushmore project. His employment was cut short when he volunteered for service with the U.S. Army during World War II.

Chief Henry Standing Bear became aware of Korczak's achievements and invited him to carve a mountain memorial to Native Americans. Ziolkowski agreed to the project after several years of discussion. He began work, using explosives to blast pieces from the mountain, on May 3, 1947. Already forty years old, he knew that he would never finish the memorial—his family would inherit the monumental task. He died in 1982 at age seventy-four, having worked on the mountain for thirty-five years.

BEST SCENIC DRIVES

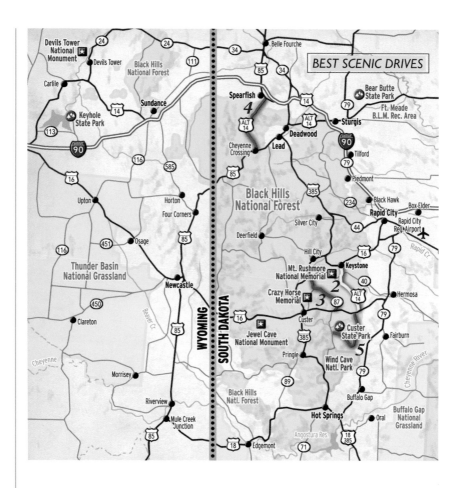

1. Badlands Loop State Scenic Highway

Distance: 61 miles
Travel time: 2 to 3 hours
The route: I-90 from Wall east to SD 240,
then south and west back to Wall

The Badlands Loop State Scenic Highway crosses a wondrous landscape of grasslands and fascinating formations. Fifty miles east of Rapid City on I-90 is the National Grasslands Visitor Center in Wall. After visiting the center, you can begin the spectacular Badlands Loop State Scenic Highway by driving east on I-90. From Wall to Exit 131, you are in a section of the Buffalo Gap National Grassland. At Exit 131, turn

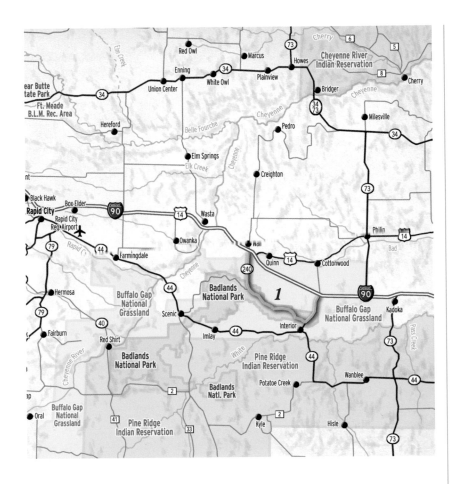

south on SD 240 and follow this road through Badlands National Park, returning to Wall and completing the loop.

Even driving at interstate speeds, the subtle beauty of the grasslands is astounding. The travel pace slows when you reach SD 240. For 31 miles, the road goes through some of the most diverse and remarkable landscapes in North America. You pass astonishing buttes, cliffs, and multicolored spires.

Walk the Cliff Shelf Trail and the Door Trail to experience the scenery up close. Now-extinct mammalian creatures once roamed the area before the badlands existed. Stop at the Fossil Exhibit Trail to see some of their 65-million-year-old remains. The Ben Reifel Visitor

Norbeck Pass, Badlands Loop, Shaina Niehans, NPS

Center is a good place to learn about the early mammoth hunters and this land that the Lakota people call home.

There are a dozen scenic overlooks where you can gaze upon the grandeur of the landscape. Many of the overlooks require a short walk from a parking area. Take your camera with you. Iconic views of the badlands are at the Big Badlands Overlook, Panorama Point, Pinnacles Overlook, and the Yellow Mounds Overlook. Inspiring photo opportunities abound.

As you tour the Badlands Loop State Scenic Highway, you might experience feelings similar to those of the acclaimed architect Frank Lloyd Wright who, upon visiting in 1935, exclaimed, "I was totally unprepared for that revelation called the Dakota Bad Lands."

2. Iron Mountain Road

Distance: 17 miles
Travel time: 45 to 60 minutes
The route: From the junction of US 16A and SD 244 south of Keystone, to the junction of US 16A and SD 36
Tunnels: Tunnel 1, 14' 0" wide by 12' 9" high, (bypass available)
Tunnel 2, 13' 2" wide by 12' 2" high, (bypass available)
Tunnel 3, 13' 4" wide by 12' 4" high, (no bypass)

Iron Mountain Road was intended to be a work of art. The scenic highway between Mount Rushmore National Memorial and Custer State Park was constructed in the 1930s, after the Needles Highway. Senator Peter Norbeck championed the road that engineers said was unbuildable. He planned a

Iron Mountain Road, ALan Leftridge

route that he declared "is not meant to be a super highway, to do the scenery justice you should drive no more than 20 mph and to do it full justice you should simply get out and walk."

Norbeck's artistic expressions are shown in the three tunnels, each one framing Mount Rushmore from a different angle, and the three "pigtail bridges," corkscrew-like structures that accommodate elevation changes while preserving the natural features. Even without these engineering marvels, Iron Mountain Road would be celebrated for its serpentine construction through remarkable Black Hills scenery.

As you drive the road you will find ample scenic turnouts and exhibits that interpret the road, Norbeck's life, and the natural history of the area.

3. Needles Highway

Distance: 14 miles
Travel time: 45 to 60 minutes
The route: From the junction of US 16 and SD 87 to the junction of SD 87 and US 16A
Tunnels: Tunnel 5, 8' 4" wide by 12' 0" high
Tunnel 6, 9' 0" wide by 12' 3" high

Needles Highway, Alan Leftridge

The Needles Highway (SD 87) is an astounding thoroughfare laid between impressive granite spires, through pine and spruce forests, and bounded by towering mountains. The roadway was named for the needle-like rock formations that pierce the sky along the highway.

What critics said was impossible to build is today a National Scenic Byway. The roadway was planned by Peter Norbeck, South Dakota governor at the time, who brilliantly scouted and marked the entire course of the road on foot and by horseback. Construction was completed the year after his term as governor in 1922.

The highway tunnels through two high granite walls. Sharp turns are in every mile. Norbeck intended the road to be traveled slowly so that it would be relished. Take your time. Stop often.

The Needles Highway is within Custer State Park, which charges an entrance fee. Along your journey, you will pass the acclaimed Needles

Eye, a unique rock formation created by rain, freezing, and thawing. The scenic byway also leads to the nationally recognized Black Hills Playhouse, beautiful Sylvan Lake, the Black Elk Peak trailhead, and numerous scenic overlooks.

Approach the road as a sightseer. Drive the length of the Needles Highway, then turn around and drive back. Catch the beauty of this unique area from different angles and note how the light changes.

4. Spearfish Canyon Scenic Byway

Distance: 19 miles
Travel time: 45 to 60 minutes
The route: Exit 10, I-90 to US 14A, then to US 85 at Cheyenne Crossing

Spearfish Canyon Scenic Byway, Alan Leftridge

Driving the Spearfish Canyon Scenic Byway is an excellent way to enter the Black Hills if you are traveling I-90. You just don't want to be in a hurry—no one else will be.

The entire distance of Spearfish Canyon is stunning. The road winds along Spearfish Creek beneath towering limestone walls and dense groves of Black Hills spruce and ponderosa pines. Deciduous trees and wildflowers hug the creek. Two of the grandest waterfalls in South Dakota are in the canyon: Bridal Veil Falls and Roughlock Falls. Sixty-foot Bridal Veil Falls is 6 miles south of Spearfish and is viewable from a platform near the road. Continue another 7 miles south to Savoy and steer right onto Roughlock Falls Road (SD 222) to reach Roughlock Falls. Here, Little Spearfish Creek tumbles 50 feet down several limestone ledges. Near both falls, look for mountain goats scaling the walls of the gorge.

Although locals enjoy Spearfish Canyon any time of the year, autumn seems to be the favorite. Quaking aspen, birch, and cottonwood trees of yellow, gold, and red adorn the gorge. The colors change daily. With an elevation change of almost 2,000 feet from Spearfish to U.S. Highway 85 at Cheyenne Crossing, you can drive from one season into the next.

Wildlife Loop Road, Custer State Park,
Chad Coppess, South Dakota Tourism

5. Wildlife Loop Road

Distance: 18 miles

Travel time: 45 minutes

The route: Looping south between SD 87 at Prairie Dog
Observation Point and US 16A just east of Game Lodge
Campground

This road twists and dips through Custer State Park's prairie and open
forest lands. It is the most popular drive in the park. People come here
with the hope of seeing the many animals that inhabit the Black Hills.

You are almost guaranteed to see animals along the road. Increase
your chances by touring when they are most active: early mornings and
evenings. Viewing opportunities are different each day, but you can expect
to see black-tailed prairie dogs and feral burros. The prairie dogs live in
colonies, some next to the roadway. The burros panhandle food along a
middle section of the road; they can't be missed.

You will also likely see some of the park's 1,300 bison. Lone bulls
strike poses against the rolling prairie backdrop. Groups of cows wander
among the wildflowers. May is calving season when the herd enlarges. In
the late spring, the cinnamon-colored newborns romp among the adults.

On most days you might see small groups of pronghorn, white-tailed deer, and mule deer. Pronghorn prefer the open prairie where they can bolt from danger. Deer stay close to the margins of prairie and forest, using the woods as cover.

Elk live both in the margins and on open prairie. Lone bulls and small groups of cows are common throughout Custer State Park. Visit in the autumn when the bulls roundup their harems. Frosty mornings are a good time to park your vehicle on a turnout and listen for the males as they "bugle" to attract the females.

Luck is with you if you glimpse bighorn sheep, coyotes, foxes, or mountain lions. They are wary.

Most visitors drive the Wildlife Loop Road to observe the park's emblematic bison and other mammals. There are other reasons to tour the byway. The warmer months feature multicolored wildflowers and stately prairie grasses on the hillsides. Songbirds, raptors, and insects are busy and entertaining.

The prairie and ponderosa pine–covered hills along Wildlife Loop Road are alive with nature's drama. Enjoy the drive at a leisurely pace.

Sturgis Motorcycle Rally

Like counting grains of sand on a beach, it is impossible to say how many motorcyclists you can find at the annual Sturgis Motorcycle Rally. Some estimates are in the hundreds of thousands. At times, the torrent of motorcycles coursing through the Black Hills is a huge spectacle. The buildup starts the first week of August and concludes at the end of the second week, with a crescendo around August 13. Although Sturgis is the center of activity, motorcycle groups schedule "runs" to various points of interest around the Black Hills during these two weeks. Even if you are not a rally participant, it is advisable to schedule your activities either to enjoy the spectacle or to avoid the crowds. For instance, you may want to plan your tour of Jewel Cave National Monument on a day when most of the events are near Sturgis or Mount Rushmore. If you visit the Black Hills at this time of year, plan ahead by accessing the official motorcycle rally schedule at www.sturgis.com.

BEST LODGES

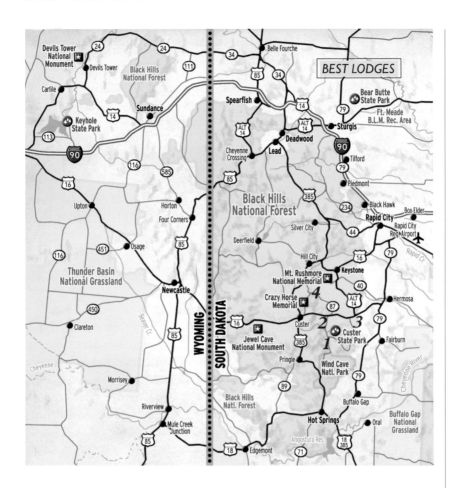

1. Blue Bell Lodge

Custer State Park offers a thematic vacation experience at the Blue Bell Lodge. The grounds are designed as a Western guest ranch. The resort offers trail rides, hayrides, chuck wagon dinners, and cowboy entertainment.

An executive of the Bell Telephone Company built the log lodge in the late 1920s. The owner named the lodge after the telephone company's logo: a blue bell. The setting is

Blue Bell Lodge, Alan Leftridge

in an open-canopy ponderosa pine forest at the base of Mount Coolidge. Custer State Park purchased the property in 1935 and has operated it since then.

The lodge stands alone as a meeting place and restaurant. Accommodations are in 29 cabins, each with an outdoor fire pit to enhance the ranch experience.

2. Legion Lake Lodge

Legion Lake has long been an attraction for visitors seeking leisure, whether for an afternoon or an extended holiday.

In 1913, several American Legion posts occupied property adjacent to Galena Creek. They also built several cabins in the

Legion Lake Lodge, Dick Kettlewell

area. The Civilian Conservation Corps built a dam across the creek in the early 1930s to form a new lake. Soon after, South Dakota purchased the land and buildings. Custer State Park Resorts later included them in its collection of historic lodges and cabins. The lake and lodge were named for the American Legion, which originally developed the area. The inn beside Legion Lake is new, constructed in 2016.

There are no guest accommodations in the lodge itself. However, scattered in the surrounding ponderosa pine forest are 26 cabins. Guests and passing visitors take advantage of the lodge's dining room, store, and recreational equipment rentals.

3. State Game Lodge

The State Game Lodge is a retreat for U.S. presidents and citizens alike. You can stay in the very rooms occupied by Presidents Coolidge and Eisenhower.

This impressive stone and wood lodge was built in 1920. It is in a lovely valley, surrounded

State Game Lodge, Alan Leftridge

by a ponderosa pine forest. A large, sloping front lawn welcomes you.

Listed on the National Register of Historic Places, a variety of accommodations are offered in the historic lodge itself, in adjacent motel-like rooms, and 24 cabins. The dining room service is one of its top attractions. You can select South Dakota specialties like buffalo, pheasant, and trout.

President Calvin Coolidge chose the State Game Lodge as his "summer White House" in 1927. His itinerary called for a three-week stay, but the serenity and beauty of the area influenced him to remain three months.

President Dwight Eisenhower was also a guest in the lodge. He stayed for three days in 1953, during a speaking engagement.

Sylvan Lake Lodge, Alan Leftridge

4. Sylvan Lake Lodge

Built in 1893, the original lodge was at the head of Sylvan Lake. You can walk the original carriage road from the Sylvan Lake parking lot to the site where the lodge burned in 1935.

The celebrated architect Frank Lloyd Wright toured the Black Hills in 1935, and upon visiting Sylvan Lake suggested the placement of today's lodge on the hill overlooking the lake.

The building has an Old World charm, with a large stone fireplace in a cozy lounge area, a rustic dining area, and an outdoor deck facing the lake below. The multi-story lodge has 35 rooms. Sprinkled along two loops are 32 cabins of various sizes.

The lodge is a 5-minute walk from Sylvan Lake where you can swim, picnic, rent watercraft items, and explore the area on foot. The Needles Highway begins near here for your touring pleasure.

BEST CAMPGROUNDS

After a day of exploring the rich beauty and grandeur of the Black Hills region, it is time to cozy up to a campfire and enjoy the evening hours. It is an Old West experience, and yet forever new—a ritual tradition of Americana.

There are dozens of privately owned, USDA Forest Service, National Park Service, and state park campgrounds in the Black Hills. Custer State Park has 10 general-use campgrounds, Badlands National Park maintains 2, Black Hills National Forest keeps 18, and Devils Tower National Monument, Bear Butte State Park, and Wind Cave National Park each have 1 campground. The campgrounds on the following list are all publicly owned. They were selected for their geographic distribution in the Black Hills, the varying recreational opportunities they present, and the high-quality experiences that each offers.

Opening and closing dates of the campgrounds are approximate. Use fees vary among campgrounds and may be adjusted seasonally. Go to the website for each administrative unit to get current camping information.

Relaxing in camp, Gary Chancey, Black Hills National Forest

Custer State Park

Blue Bell Campground

Camp in an open, park-like ponderosa pine forest while enjoying this full-service campground. The Blue Bell area operates as a small dude ranch, with all of the amenities that you would expect. Blue Bell is a favorite campground for families looking for outdoor adventures close at hand.

- Season: April 29 to October 31.
- Reservations: Accepted one year in advance, www.campsd.com.
- 31 sites, 23 camping cabins.
- Facilities: Flush toilets with showers, drinking water, laundromat, store, gift shop, restaurant, horseback riding, hayrides, and chuck wagon cookouts.

Center Lake Campground

This campground has plenty of shaded sites, some along the creek and others above the lake in ponderosa pine woodlands.

🪰 Season: April 29 to September 30.

🪰 Reservations: Same-day reservations, www.campsd.com.

🪰 71 sites, no electricity.

🪰 Facilities: Vault toilets, showers, swimming beach, and boat dock.

Game Lodge Campground

This campground is a short walking distance to the State Game Lodge with a full-service restaurant, bar, and gift shop. A few steps beyond the lodge is a snack bar, gift shop, and a store with camp supplies.

🪰 Season: Open year-round with different seasonal services.

🪰 Reservations: Same-day reservations, www.campsd.com.

🪰 59 sites, 11 camper cabins. Electric service for ADA visitors.

🪰 Facilities: Flush and vault toilets, showers, drinking water, RV waste dumpsite, laundry, playground, swimming, and fishing pond.

🪰 ADA accessible sites.

Legion Lake Campground

This campground is north of U.S. Highway 16 and a short walk from spectacular Legion Lake. In a heavily forested area, the campground accommodates mostly RV units, with 5 sites specified for tents.

🪰 Season: May 13 to September 30.

🪰 Reservations: www.campsd.com.

🪰 26 sites, lodge cabins.

🪰 Facilities: Flush toilets, showers, drinking water, electric hookups, playground, paddleboard and kayak rentals, fishing dock, store, snack bar, restaurant, and Legion Lake Lodge.

🪰 ADA accessible fishing dock.

Sylvan Lake Campground

This very popular campground is 0.25-mile southeast of Sylvan Lake at the beginning of the scenic Needles Highway.

🪰 Season: May 27 to September 30.

🪰 Reservations: www.campsd.com.

🪰 39 sites. Not suitable for RVs over 27 feet or large tents. Some hike-in sites.

🪰 Facilities: Flush toilets and showers, vault toilets, drinking water. Within easy walking distance are a playground, gift shop, fishing dock, store, restaurant, cafeteria, snack bar, picnic area, and trail access.

Grace Coolidge Campground

This campground in the trees along babbling Grace Coolidge Creek is divided by U.S. Highway 16A. The north side is for tents only, and the south side allows all kinds of camping units. Expect to see wildlife in the campground. Grace Coolidge Walk-In Fishing Area is an easy walk from the campground.

- Season: May 20 to October 17.
- Reservations: www.campsd.com.
- 27 sites, multiple use and tents only.
- Facilities: Flush toilets, showers, and drinking water.

Stockade South Campground

Stockade South is a small Custer State Park campground with several camping cabins. It is close to Custer, making it easy to get supplies. It is a convenient base from which to explore Custer State Park.

Stockade Lake, Chad Coppess, South Dakota Tourism

- Season: May 20 to September 30.
- Reservations: Available one year in advance, www.campsd.com.
- 23 campsites, 13 cabins.
- Facilities: Flush toilets, showers, and drinking water.

Black Hills National Forest

Bismarck Lake Campground

The CCC constructed this campground in the 1930s with spacious sites, most with open views of the small, pristine lake. Your site will be in a beautiful mixed ponderosa pine–aspen forest. A well-marked trail system circles the lake and leads to an overlook of neighboring Stockdale Lake.

- Season: Open year-round.
- First-come, first-served, or call (877) 444-6777 for reservations.
- 23 sites, several can be reserved.
- Facilities: Pit toilets and drinking water.
- ADA accessibility: 5 campsites and trail system.

Roubaix Lake Campground

Campsites are scattered among four loops in a ponderosa pine forest along the shoreline of small, secluded Roubaix Lake. Some sites have lake views. The campground is quiet and well maintained. The multiple recreation opportunities that abound in the area make this a popular campground. It is a perfect place to serve as a base camp for area day hikes, mountain biking, canoeing, kayaking, horseback riding, swimming, and fishing.

- Season: Open year-round.
- First-come, first-served.
- 56 sites.
- Facilities: Pit toilets and drinking water.

Horsethief Lake Campground

This quiet campground has a secluded feel yet is close to everything the central hills have to offer: Crazy Horse, Mount Rushmore, and Custer State Park. The campground is peaceful and spread out. The tent sites are large, in a valley, away from the RVs.

- Season: May 24 to September 4.
- Reservations: 4 days ahead of arrival.
- 36 sites.
- Facilities: Vault toilets, drinking water, electricity, store, laundry, trail access, fishing, and lake access.

Sheridan Lake South Shore Campground

Smokey, Rocky, Chipper, Thumper, and Woodsey are the names of the loops in this campground. The campsites in Rocky Loop are large and offer the most solitude.

- Season: May 24 to September 4.
- Reservations: www.recreation.gov or (877-444-6777).
- 126 sites.
- Facilities: Vault toilets, drinking water, beach, and boat rental.

Grizzly Creek Campground

This small campground is an option for campers preferring a tenting-only experience. The campsites along the creek are the best. You will hear a lot of songbirds because the campground is in the Peter Norbeck Wildlife Preserve.

- Season: Open the weekend before Memorial Day through the weekend after Labor Day.
- First-come, first-served.
- 19 sites, tents only.
- Facilities: Vault toilets and drinking water.

Hanna Campground

This campground offers a beautiful, peaceful setting along a fork of Spearfish Creek. One section of the campground is in an open meadow while the second area is in a mature spruce forest. Near the community of Cheyenne Crossing, it is a good choice for exploring nearby Spearfish Canyon, and an excellent place to find solitude.

- Season: Open the weekend before Memorial Day through the weekend after Labor Day.
- Walk-in tent sites are open year-round.
- First-come, first-served.
- 13 sites.
- Facilities: Vault toilets, drinking water, and a 1-mile loop nature trail.

Reuter Campground

This small campground is near Sundance, Wyoming. The campground has two loops on a hillside covered with ponderosa pines. There is an extensive trail system in the Sundance area. This campground makes a good base camp for exploring the northwest area of the Black Hills region.

- Season: Open from snowmelt to snowfall.
- Reservations: www.recreation.gov or (877-444-6777).
- 24 sites.
- Facilities: Vault toilets and water.

Bear Butte State Park

Bear Butte Lake Campground

This small campground is across the highway at the north end of Bear Butte Lake. All sites are non-electric and are available on a first-come, first-served basis. The campground has excellent views of Bear Butte with the glistening lake in the foreground.

- Season: Open year-round.
- 15 sites.
- Facilities: Flush toilets and drinking water, late May to late September. Pit toilets and no water in the off-season.

Devils Tower National Monument

Belle Fourche River Campground

Two campground loops stretch among towering cottonwoods along the Belle Fourche River. If you just want to picnic, shelters and tables are north of the campground.

- Season: May through October.
- First-come, first-served.
- 50 sites, 4 accessible, 3 for groups.
- Facilities: Accessible flush toilets and drinking water.

Wind Cave National Park

Elk Mountain Campground

Enjoy staying in the beautiful mixed grasslands, watching wildlife, observing the flora, and star gazing. The campground has four loops with spacious sites. It is an excellent choice for a quiet camping experience if you want to be close to Wind Cave or away from the crowds in Custer State Park.

- Season: Open year-round.
- First-come, first-served.
- 62 sites
- Facilities: Flush toilets and drinking water through warmer months. Pit toilets and no water in the off-season.

Badlands National Park

Sage Creek Campground

If you love sunrises, sunsets, and dark starlit nights, then Sage Creek is

Relaxing, Chad Coppess, South Dakota Tourism

where you want to stay. Sage Creek is a primitive campground, accessed by an unpaved road. You will see many bison along the road and in the campground. You are in their habitat. Plan to arrive early to get a good spot with a table in this quiet, sagebrush-dotted meadow.

- Season: Open year-round, but the road may close due to weather.
- First-come, first-served.
- 30+ sites.
- Facilities: Pit toilets. No water available, bring your own.

Cedar Pass Campground

This campground is near the Ben Reifel Visitor Center and campground store. Campsites have unobstructed great views of the surrounding badlands, and clear nights offer incredible dark skies for star gazing. Park interpreters conduct evening presentations in the nearby amphitheater. Cedar Pass can be a busy campground; get reservations and try for a site close to the grasslands.

- Season: Open year-round.
- Reservations: First-come, first-served, or make reservations at (877) 386-4383 or www.cedarpasslodge.com.
- 96 sites.
- Facilities: Flush toilets, showers, drinking water, electricity, and RV dump station.
- ADA accessible sites.

Current Campground Information

Changing conditions occur due to weather, visitation load, and construction projects. Avoid surprises and plan ahead by getting up-to-date information about your campground choice.

Custer State Park www.campsd.com (800) 710-2267	Bear Butte State Park www.campsd.com (605) 347-5240
Black Hills National Forest www.fs.usda.gov/activity/blackhills (605) 673-9200	Badlands National Park www.cedarpasslodge.com (605) 433-5460
Wind Cave National Park www.nps.gov/wica (605) 745-4600 or (605) 745-1134	Devils Tower National Monument www.nps.gov/deto (307) 467-5283

BEST PICNIC AREAS

To find the best picnic areas in the Black Hills, look for water. Streams, rivers, and lakes provide wonderful settings for recreation and scenic pleasure. There are dozens of picnic spots on public and private lands throughout the region. Popular picnic areas are by the Belle Fourche River, Spearfish Creek, Rapid Creek, Center Lake, Legion Lake, Pactola Lake, Horsethief Lake, and Sylvan Lake.

Stockade Lake, Chad Coppess, South Dakota Tourism

Review a map of the Black Hills and decide what water resource you want to be near at picnic time. You will likely find a spot that provides all your scenic and recreational needs.

BEST HIKES

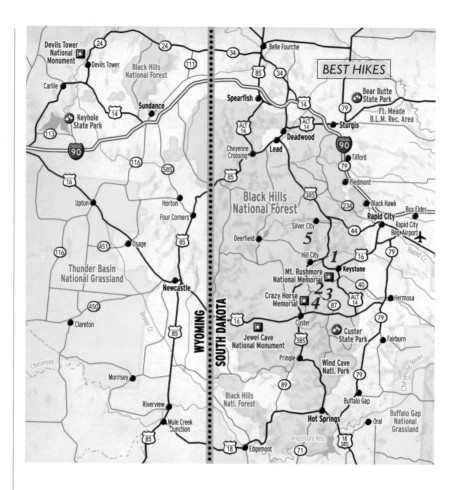

Hiking in the Black Hills,
Chad Coppess, South Dakota Tourism

The Black Hills region is a hiker's playground. There are more than 450 trails, offering everything from easy strolls on paved surfaces to scrambling over shattered rocks up rugged peaks. Because the area is big and diverse, it can be difficult to select the best places to take a short walk. There are several trails that I consider the best for offering you a flavor of the Black Hills. This section lists five trails. Other hikes are listed in the section on Best Iconic Places. I encourage you to discover the natural and cultural heritage of the Black Hills by foot. Hikes reward your explorations of meadows, forests, and prairies. Tour the region by vehicle, but also experience the sights, sounds, and fragrances of the Black Hills on a hike.

Be Prepared

Mountain weather is fickle. A bright summer morning can become a bitter, wet, and windy afternoon. Take layers of warm, water-repellent clothing, hiking shoes, plenty of water, first-aid equipment, insect repellent, and maps. It is easy to become disoriented in the mountains. Stay on the trails!

For your added pleasure, I suggest that you take a snack on all of your hikes. Carry an extra bag to pack out your litter. Keep in mind that discarded orange peels, apple cores, sunflower seed husks, and pistachio shells take many years to deteriorate in the wild, plus they are unsightly and do not benefit wildlife. Enjoy the backcountry, and help keep the land as pristine as you found it.

1. Spring Creek Trail

Hiking in the Black Hills,
Chad Coppess, South Dakota Tourism

Level of difficulty: Easy
Duration: 2 hours
Distance: 2.7-mile loop
Elevation change: Minimal
Best time of the year: Spring through fall
Trailhead: From Hill City, drive 7 miles east on US 385 and turn onto County Road 228. This road becomes Sheridan Lake Road. Follow it 3 miles to the Upper Spring Creek Trailhead on the right.

Notes: The hike joins a section of the Flume Trail, an excellent discovery trail for all levels of hikers. It is a National Recreation Trail because of its significant cultural heritage. The trail follows part of the Rockerville Flume, which during the early 1880s carried water 20 miles from Spring Creek to the placer excavations near Rockerville. You will discover mining artifacts, tunnels, and abundant wildlife along your hike.

The hike: At the trailhead, take the right-hand trail. You will begin a slow descent toward Sheridan Lake along Spring Creek. This trail is incredibly diverse and takes you through beautiful scenery. There are several stream crossings that may be nearly dry in mid- to late summer.

At 1 mile you reach the intersection of Trail #50 from Sheridan Lake and the Calumet Trailhead. Turn left and follow this trail. This part of the loop is a section of the historic Flume Trail.

Within 0.5 mile the trail goes through a tunnel then meanders 0.25 mile to a left turn back to the Upper Spring Creek Trailhead. Alternatively, you may wish to continue another 0.25 mile beyond this point to investigate a second tunnel. If you do, you will need to backtrack to the trail junction that returns you to your vehicle.

2. Black Elk Peak Trail

Level of difficulty: Moderate
Duration: 4 to 5 hours
Distance: 7.0-mile loop
Elevation change: 1,100-foot elevation gain/loss
Best time of the year: Spring through fall

Black Elk Peak, Beth Doten, Black Hills National Forest

Trailhead: The trail begins at the Sylvan Lake Day Use Area in Custer State Park. Select Trail #4 at Sylvan Lake to Black Elk Peak, returning to Sylvan Lake by way of Trail #9.

Notes: Black Elk Peak Trail leads you to an abandoned fire lookout on the top of the highest mountain in the Black Hills. This trail is one of the most popular in the Black Hills. Expect plenty of fellow hikers, regardless of the season. Select Trail #9 for your return and you will avoid the direct afternoon sun. Take plenty of water and snacks, regardless of when you travel. Choose a clear day to get the best long-distance views. Expect windy conditions on top.

The hike: Trail #4 begins as an easy walk through a ponderosa pine forest and big boulders. After meeting the Little Devils Tower Trailhead on SD 87, the trail bends to the northeast and soon climbs and eventually connects with the Peter Norbeck Trail #3. Go left on Trail #3 to a junction with Trail #9. Continue north on Trail #9; the last mile is steep as you climb toward the summit.

At the top you are rewarded with fantastic views. And you just hiked to the highest point in the United States east of the Rocky Mountains!

Explore the historic fire tower. Look for the backside of Mount Rushmore and the Badlands from the observation area.

Return to your car by retracing your steps down Trail #9. Stay on this trail as it descends through ponderosa pine forest and towering blocks of granite to the trailhead at Sylvan Lake.

3. Sunday Gulch Trail

Level of difficulty: Moderate to strenuous

Duration: 3 hours

Distance: 3.0-mile loop

Elevation change: 330 feet

Best time of the year: Year-round

Trailhead: The Sunday Gulch Trail begins behind the dam at Sylvan Lake in Custer State Park. Park at the large lot near the general store along SD 87, inside the west entrance to Custer State Park. Walk west around Sylvan Lake to the trailhead.

Notes: Sunday Gulch Trail is a favorite loop off the Sylvan Lakeshore Trail. It

Sunday Gulch,
Chad Coppess, South Dakota Tourism

winds through a ponderosa pine and spruce forest, crossing a stream in several places. Be careful on the wet, slippery rocks. Prepare to remove your shoes and socks if you do not have outdoor hiking sandals. The cold water can be knee deep.

The hike: The beginning of this hike is challenging as the trail quickly descends into the gulch and you meet the first of several stream crossings. Steps and handrails keep you from slipping. Once in the gulch, the trail hugs the creek and granite walls. Your walk will be cool, mossy, and quiet. After several stream crossings, the trail begins a strenuous climb to Sylvan Lake. Follow the shoreline path back to the trailhead.

4. Little Devils Tower

Level of difficulty: Moderate to mildly strenuous

Duration: 4 hours

Distance: 3.1 miles round trip

Elevation change: 700-foot elevation gain/loss

Best time of the year: Spring through fall

Trailhead: The trailhead is on the north side of SD 87, 0.5 mile east of Sylvan Lake in Custer State Park.

Notes: Follow the blue-blazed markers along Trail #4. The path is heavily used in the summer months and easy to follow.

The hike: The first part the trail snakes through a Black Hills spruce forest and around huge boulders. Continue following the blue markers uphill. The last section of the trail is steep and requires you to scramble over broken rocks and through clefts in boulders. Watch for mountain goats in this part of the trail. The 6,926-foot summit of Little Devils Tower provides views of the Cathedral Spires, the backside of Mount Rushmore, the town of Custer, and nearby Black Elk Peak.

Near Little Devils Tower,
Chad Coppess, South Dakota Tourism

5. George S. Mickelson Trail

Level of difficulty: Easy to moderate
Duration: 5 days
Distance: 109 miles one way
Elevation change: 330 feet
Best time of the year: Year-round
Trailhead: There are 14 trailheads along the Mickelson Trail.
Notes: The Mickelson Trail is South Dakota's first rails-to-trails project. It follows a converted railroad bed running between Edgemont and Deadwood. The pathway is crushed rock and wide to accommodate equestrians, hikers, mountain bikers, snowmobilers, and cross-country skiers. The trail has 100 bridges and 4 tunnels along the route. It passes through Black Hills National Forest and privately owned land. You can choose to walk the entire distance over several days or gain access to the trail at any of the 14 trailheads.

Trestle on the Mickelson Trail, Chad Coppess, South Dakota Tourism

The hike: The heart of the Black Hills is open to you along this route as it threads through national forest and private lands. In residential areas, the rail line tends to pass between backyards, giving you a glimpse of what it's like to live in the rural Black Hills.

The trail's northern section skirts mountains and ponderosa pine forests and threads over creeks and through narrow valleys from Deadwood to Lead, Rochford, and Mystic. Every few miles it traverses a converted railroad bridge on trestles hundreds of feet high. South of Mystic, a once-thriving mining town, a 40-foot-long tunnel passes through the heart of the Precambrian-age core of the Black Hills. From Hill City south to Custer, the landscape slowly changes from mountains and ponderosa pine to meadows and prairie. You will find many tourist sites nearby, including the Crazy Horse Memorial and Mount Rushmore.

From Custer south, you pass outcroppings with multicolored lichens growing on the rocks. Two concrete bridges will stand out because all of the other bridges are wooden.

You will see a few of the railroad mile markers made of heavy metal, painted white, and printed with the distance number to the nearest one-hundredth of a mile. Old telegraph poles and concrete fence posts line the way.

The vegetation becomes more varied the closer you get to Edgemont. The high country supplies water to cottonwood, boxelder, plum trees, chokecherries, and sagebrush.

Ponderosa pines are common by the time you reach the Cheyenne River overlook. The southern section of the trail is characterized by prairie grasses and the animals that the vegetation supports: prairie dogs, deer, pronghorn, bison, and domestic cattle.

TRAIL ETIQUETTE

You may find total solitude on your hike, but chances are you will meet others. Consider the following while on the trail:

- *Take time to acknowledge other hikers. Say hello, and exchange information about trail conditions, wildlife, and scenery.*
- *Stay on the trail; cutting switchbacks and making shortcuts causes erosion.*
- *Always yield to uphill hikers. Show courtesy by stepping aside and allowing hikers traveling uphill to keep their pace.*
- *Equestrians share many of the trails with hikers. When encountering a mounted horse, step off the trail to the downhill side.*
- *Apple cores, banana skins, nut and seed shells, and orange peels are human food scraps. None belong in wildlife diets. Refrain from littering with these and other food items, thinking that animals will appreciate the nourishment. The scraps are slow to decompose, are unsightly, and are unhealthy for wildlife.*
- *Leave no trace that you visited.*

Breezy Point, Black Hills, Chad Coppess, South Dakota Tourism

BEST BICYCLE RIDES

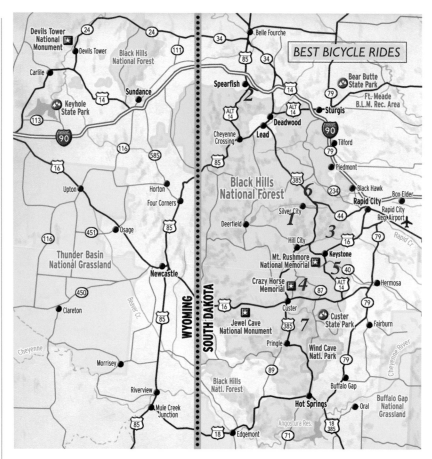

The Black Hills region is rich in biking opportunities on abandoned logging roads, U.S. Forest Service roads, highways, municipal bikeways, and trails. Road and tour bikers alike love the wide shoulders and uniform gradients of most of the Black Hills' highways. You will find what you want in the Black Hills, whether you seek a leisurely ride or an extreme challenge.

The most popular biking trails and scenic roadways are:

Mountain biking, Chad Coppess, South Dakota Tourism

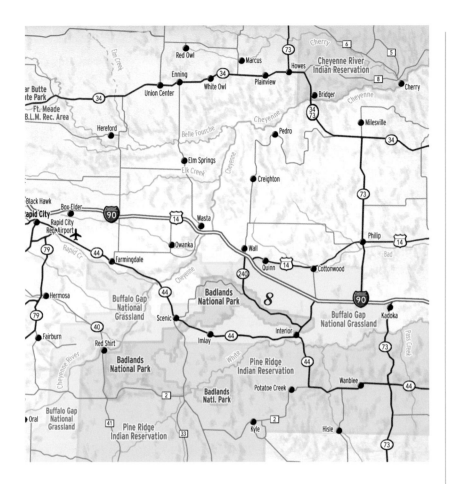

1. George S. Mickelson Trail

The Mickelson Trail passes through some of the most outstanding beauty in the Black Hills. It runs north and south between Deadwood and Edgemont, near Hot Springs, following an old railroad bed. The 109-mile trail surface is crushed limestone and gravel, making it an easy ride. You can access the trail at any of the 14 trailheads along the route. If you

Mickelson Trail, Chad Coppess, South Dakota Tourism

were to travel the entire distance, you would ride through 4 tunnels and across 100 converted railroad bridges.

Cycling in the Black Hills, Gary Chancey, Black Hills National Forest

2. Spearfish Canyon

This 12.6-mile ride follows US 14A through spectacular Spearfish Canyon. Once hailed by *Bicycling Magazine* as one of the top 50 scenic bike rides in the country, this route runs from Spearfish to Savoy with a 1,215-foot elevation gain. The ride begins in Spearfish on a paved bike path heading south from the junction of Winterville Drive and South Canyon Street. In less than a mile, the path joins US 14A, where cyclists enjoy a 4-foot-wide bike lane on the shoulder. You will ride by Bridal Veil Falls, and at Savoy you can continue another mile to Roughlock Falls.

3. Centennial Trail #89

Bicyclists, hikers, and horseback riders prize this 111-mile trail between Bear Butte State Park in the north and Wind Cave National Park in the south. This moderate trail has a few portions that require a small fee. Fee information may be obtained at any of the 21 trailheads. Also, some short sections are closed to bicycles, but there are bypasses for cyclists.

Tunnel on Needles Highway, Alan Leftridge

4. Needles Highway

The Needles National Scenic Byway (SD 87) is a narrow, paved, two-lane road that runs 14 miles between US 385 and US 16A. You will encounter narrow tunnels and several hairpin curves. The byway is famous for its incredible granite spires and the Needles Eye. You will ride by beautiful Sylvan Lake, a great place to explore on foot.

5. Iron Mountain Road

Serpentine Iron Mountain Road (a section of US 16A) has 314 curves, 14 switchbacks, 3 tunnels, and 3 "pigtail bridges." It was constructed through a ponderosa pine forest, winding around trees and boulders. You will not encounter fast vehicles. The road is paved but was designed to keep the speed limit under 35 miles per hour. The 17 miles of this scenic wonder run between SD 244 and SD 36.

6. U.S. Highway 385

More commonly known as the Black Hills Parkway, this 87-mile paved route is the longest road in the Black Hills. Riding on a wide shoulder, you will pass through several tourist sites and communities, including Hot Springs, Wind Cave National Park, Custer, Crazy Horse Memorial, Hill City, Pactola Lake, Roubaix Lake, Lead, and Deadwood.

7. Wildlife Loop Road

Custer State Park's 18-mile, paved Wildlife Loop Road is a rolling byway through forests and prairie grasslands. Traveling the road is a good way to see bison, prairie dogs, pronghorn, and burros.

8. Badlands Loop State Scenic Byway

This 22-mile section of the scenic byway takes you through the eastern section of Badlands National Park from Pinnacles Overlook east to either the Ben Reifel Visitor Center, or add another 8 miles north to the Big Badlands Overlook. The paved road is winding and undulating, with turnouts to stop and enjoy the scenic rock formations and multicolored buttes. Several foot trails lead from the road to spectacular views.

Cyclist in Badlands NP, NPS photo

BEST HORSEBACK RIDES

Experience traveling through the Black Hills as early settlers did. Several concessionaires operate horseback rides in different areas of the Black Hills. Each area has its own scenery, historic sites, stories, fauna, and flora for you to discover. Select a stable near where you are staying. Rides last from one hour to all day and cater to a range of riding abilities.

Pausing for a drink, Gary Chancey, Black Hills National Forest

Custer

Blue Bell Stables
12878 North Lame Johnny Road
Custer, SD 57730
(605) 255-4700

Hollingsworth Horses
Stagg Road
Custer, SD 57730
(605) 517-0860

Rockin' R Rides
24853 Village Avenue
Custer, SD 57730
(605) 673-2999

Keystone

Triple R Ranch
13201 Greyhound Gulch Road
Keystone, SD 57751
(605) 666-4605

Hill City

The Stables at Palmer Gulch
12620 SD Hwy 244
(605) 574-3412

Lead

Andy's Trail Rides
11264 US Hwy 14A
Lead, SD 57754
(605) 645-2211

Telephone the stables for reservations and for specifics on ages, times, distances, and prices. Don't forget your hat!

BEST BOATING

The Black Hills have several popular boating lakes. You can bring your own boat or rent a watercraft to explore these sparkling waters.

Pactola Lake is the largest lake in the Black Hills. You can rent canoes, power boats, and pontoon boats to cruise this 800-acre gem.

Sheridan Lake Marina has a wide variety of boat rentals for you to explore this 383-acre lake.

If you have not brought your own watercraft, a Sylvan Lake concessionaire has canoes and paddleboards for rent.

Deerfield Lake, at 435 acres, and Center Lake, just off Playhouse Road, are both no-wake lakes, making them perfect for canoeing, kayaking, and paddleboarding.

Kayaking on Sheridan Lake,
Gary Chancey, Black Hills National Forest

The Legion Lake concessionaire has both kayaks and paddleboards for rent to explore this beautiful lake.

Locals find small Bismarck Lake a popular place for kayaking, paddleboarding, and canoeing.

These seven lakes offer the best Black Hills water sports activities. Whatever your itinerary, there is a lake nearby for you to explore.

BEST LAKES

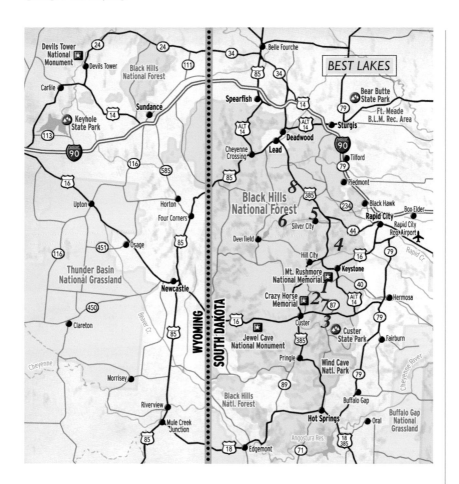

Do you love lake scenery? If so, the Black Hills offer you many opportunities to fall in love. All of the lakes listed here are easily accessible by road. They were selected for this section for their popularity to locals and vacationers alike. Each is in stunningly beautiful mountainous terrain. Several have campgrounds or

Horsethief Lake, Beth Steinhauer, Black Hills National Forest

accommodations nearby for you to extend your stay. Plan to visit all eight, and choose the scenery that you like best.

1. Horsethief Lake

Next to SD 244 and close to Mount Rushmore National Memorial, sits a 16-acre prismatic treasure amid rounded boulders and a pine forest. The photogenic lake is named after a band of horse thieves that operated out of the area long ago.

2. Sylvan Lake

Sylvan Lake, Alan Leftridge

Considered Custer State Park's crown jewel, Sylvan Lake is one of the most breathtaking lakes in South Dakota. The 17-acre lake was created in 1881 when a dam was built across Sunday Gulch. The immediate surroundings offer picnicking, rock climbing, hiking trails, swimming, small watercraft rentals, and a general store. You can walk around the lake to enjoy its beautiful setting, surrounded by ponderosa pines and picturesque granite rock formations.

Legion Lake, Chad Coppess, South Dakota Tourism

3. Legion Lake

The Civilian Conservation Corps built a dam across Galena Creek in the early 1930s to form this 9-acre beauty. Legion Lake is a popular area, offering amazing scenery and a short trail around the water's edge. It is a great family place for swimming, picnicking, fishing, and non-motorized boating. Legion Lake Lodge is next to the lake, offering boat rentals, a snack bar, and a general store. The lakeshore has an ADA accessible fishing platform.

4. Sheridan Lake

This 383-acre lake was created in 1940 as a recreational lake by the Civilian Conservation Corps. The lake area has picnic areas, hiking trails, sandy swimming beaches, a marina, and two campgrounds. The lake is popular for fishing, picnicking, hiking, boating, and camping.

Beach at Sheridan Lake, Gary Chancey, Black Hills National Forest

5. Pactola Lake

Completed in 1956, Pactola Dam formed 800-acre Pactola Lake, the largest reservoir in the Black Hills. Nestled in a rugged valley, the views from high points around the lake are stunning. Pactola Lake is famous for boating, fishing, and swimming (use footwear, the rocks are sharp). Services ashore include boat rentals (pontoon and power boats, and canoes) and hiking trails.

Pactola Lake, Chad Coppess, South Dakota Tourism

6. Deerfield Lake

This 435-acre reservoir lies among limestone outcroppings. The lake was formed by damming Castle Creek, making it the second-largest body of water in the Black Hills. The developed complex around the lake includes three campgrounds, two boat launches, two picnic areas,

Deerfield Lake, Beth Steinhauer, Black Hills National Forest

and the Deerfield Lake Loop Trail. Deerfield is a no-wake lake, making it perfect for canoeing, kayaking, and paddleboarding. It is popular for year-round angling. Trout grow quickly, feeding on abundant crayfish, and are relatively easy to catch.

7. Bismarck Lake

Ponderosa pine and aspen growing among beautiful granite boulders surround this 27-acre lake. The lakeshore trail system accommodates strollers, wheelchairs, and walkers. A simple trail leads to the south end of the lake, and can be extended to a full loop along the shoreline. Camping, fishing, kayaking, paddleboarding, and canoeing are popular water sports at this family-friendly lake.

8. Roubaix Lake

Kayaking, canoeing, fishing, and swimming from a large sandy beach are favorite activities at this 6-acre lake. Surrounded by ponderosa pines, Roubaix Lake has a large campground that attracts locals and vacationers alike.

BEST FISHING

Anglers love to come to the Black Hills because lake and stream fishing opportunities abound. Dozens of mountain lakes and many miles of streams offer choices for those who prefer fishing with dry flies, lures, or live bait. Angling is a year-round pleasure, from early spring runoff stream fishing to mid-winter ice fishing. The Black Hills' waters offer enjoyment for every age and angling ability.

Cold trout, Gary Chancey, Black Hills National Forest

In 1886, the only fish known to exist in the Black Hills were suckers, chubs, and dace. Thanks to stocking programs, trout are now found in lakes and streams throughout the Black Hills. According to the South Dakota Department of Game, Fish, and Parks, "If it looks like there is enough water for a trout to swim, then the stream or lake is worth fishing."

Find your best hot spot and enjoy!

Lake Fishing

The Black Hills hold about 22 lakes and reservoirs large enough for angling-size fish. The larger fishable lakes that are easy to access, and the populations of game fish within each, include:

Fishing at Horsethief Lake, Beth Steinhauer, Black Hills National Forest

Horsethief Lake: rainbow trout
Sheridan Lake: brown trout, northern pike, and yellow perch
Stockade Lake: yellow perch, largemouth bass, and smallmouth bass
Bear Butte Lake: bullheads, crappies, and northern pike
Deerfield Lake: brook trout, rainbow trout, and splake
Castle Creek Lake: brook trout and brown trout
Lakota Lake: rainbow trout
Roubaix Lake: brook trout and rainbow trout
Bismarck Lake: rainbow trout and yellow perch
Pactola Lake: rainbow trout, brown trout, and lake trout
Canyon Lake: rainbow trout and brown trout

Legion Lake: rainbow trout
Sylvan Lake: rainbow trout
Center Lake: rainbow trout
Iron Creek Lake: yellow perch, rainbow trout, and brown trout

Stream Fishing

There are more than 800 miles of managed streams in the Black Hills. Stretched end-to-end they would reach from Minneapolis to Denver. Almost all have populations of trout. Most streams are stocked year-round. The best-known waterways, and the fish that inhabit them, are:

Fly fishing on Spring Creek, Gary Chancey, Black Hills National Forest

Spearfish Creek: rainbow trout, brown trout, and brook trout
Whitewood Creek: brown trout
Spring Creek: brown trout
Spring Creek tributaries: brook trout
French Creek: brown trout
Rapid Creek: brown trout
Grace Coolidge Creek: brook trout, rainbow trout, and brown trout
Crow Creek: brown trout
Grizzly Bear Creek: brook trout
Castle Creek: brown trout
Battle Creek: brook trout
Iron Creek: brook trout

Most of these streams lose water as summer progresses. The central core of the Black Hills, where many streams originate, is impermeable granite. As the water flows downhill, it is absorbed as it passes over porous limestone. Some of these streams will be dry at lower elevations by September.

Fly fishing, Chad Coppess, South Dakota Tourism

BEST FISH

The Black Hills region is prized for its variety of fishing opportunities. Within a relatively small area there are eleven reservoirs plus the Belle Fourche River, Spring Creek, Spearfish Creek, and Rapid Creek. Collectively they offer year-round opportunities to catch largemouth and smallmouth bass, walleye, bluegill, perch, pike, catfish, brown trout, cutthroat trout, rainbow trout, and brook trout.

If you prefer trout, the streams and some lakes provide ample opportunities to cast a fly. Fly fishing is the most popular method for catching trout. Envelope yourself in the splendid Black Hills scenery while testing your luck. Be sure to pick up a copy of the South Dakota Fishing Handbook for current regulations and purchase a state fishing license online or at local stores. To prevent the spread of invasive aquatic species and diseases, visitors from outside the area should carefully clean and dry their gear—waders, wading shoes, float tubes, etc.—before fishing in the Black Hills.

Brook trout, NPS photo

Brook Trout
Salvelinus fontinalis

Brook trout depend on well-oxygenated, cold, clear, pure water. They are a popular sport fish for anglers who prefer fly fishing and enjoy casting their lines under tree branches into deeply shaded habitats.

Brookies are native to the northeastern United States and the Appalachian Mountains south to Georgia. They have been widely introduced to non-native waters and now inhabit lakes, river, streams, creeks, and ponds throughout the West. In many non-native waters, brook trout are considered invasive, competing with populations of native fish such as cutthroat trout.

Best Place to Find Brook Trout
Brook trout are common in Deerfield Lake and Spearfish Creek.

Brown trout, NPS photo

Brown Trout
Salmo trutta

Brown trout are a European species—a native of Germany—brought to the United States in the late 1800s. Reclusive and wily, browns have become one of the most sought-after fish among fly-fishing enthusiasts. Brown trout prosper in cold streams, rivers, and lakes. They prefer deeper habitats near the streambed, rather than near the water surface. Anglers will find that the Black Hills offer ideal places for them to test their skills, or try their luck.

Best Place to Find Brown Trout
Brown trout are found in most streams in the Black Hills, including Rapid Creek, Spearfish Creek, and French Creek. Anglers will also find them in Canyon Lake, Pactola Reservoir, Deerfield Lake, and Sylvan Lake.

Cutthroat trout, Jay Fleming, NPS photo

Cutthroat Trout
Oncorhynchus clarkii

Explorer Meriwether Lewis of the Lewis and Clark Expedition first chronicled the existence of cutthroat trout as a distinct species while he was navigating the Missouri River near Great Falls. Today, cutthroats are found in less than half their native range, though they have also been introduced to waters in Virginia, Michigan, Arkansas, Arizona, and elsewhere.

Cutthroat trout prefer well-oxygenated, small-to-large, clear, shallow rivers with gravelly bottoms. They are prized by anglers as a favorite gamefish.

Best Place to Find Cutthroat Trout
In the northeast corner of the Black Hills (in Wyoming), Sand Creek contains a remnant population of resident cutthroats. Rumor has it that cutts may still swim in a few other Black Hills streams—when you hook a trout, look for the cutt's characteristic red-orange slash beneath the jaw.

Rainbow Trout
Oncorhynchus mykiss

Rainbow trout, NPS photo

Native to the coldwater streams of western North America, rainbow trout populations in the Black Hills region occur in small rocky streams. They prefer to feed near the water's surface in open runs. Rainbow are also stocked annually in many of the lakes and reservoirs here. Like brook trout, the average life expectancy of rainbow trout is about four years.

Best Place to Find Rainbow Trout
Rainbow trout are common in Whitewood, French, and Spearfish Creeks and in Deerfield Lake, Pactola Reservoir, Sheridan Lake, Canyon Lake, and Sylvan Lake.

BEST HISTORIC SITES

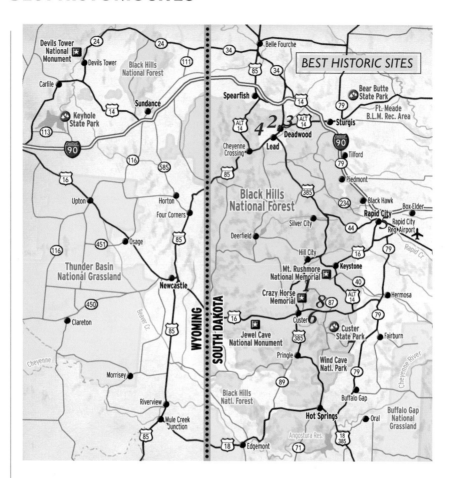

1. Black Elk Peak Fire Lookout Tower

The Civilian Conservation Corps constructed the fire lookout tower on Black Elk Peak in 1938 (when it was known as Harney Peak). All of the building materials, including stones, were hauled the 3.5 miles up the mountain by horse-drawn carts. The CCC provided the occupants with living space, running water, heat, and electricity. The tower sits atop the highest point in the Black Hills, where staff would

Black Elk Peak Fire Lookout Tower,
Gary Chancey, Black Hills National Forest

scan the forests for smoke. Today, the lookout is no longer used for fire spotting, and visitors can enter the tower to enjoy fantastic views—after the moderate uphill hike.

2. Bullock Hotel

The famous Bullock Hotel stands at 633 Main Street in Deadwood. Seth Bullock and Sol Star built the three-story, white and pink sandstone hotel for $40,000 on the site where their warehouse burned in 1894. They designed a sixty-three-room luxury hotel with steam heat, a library, parlor, and a bathroom on each floor. The restaurant could seat 100, and diners could select lobster and pheasant as main courses.

When you enter the large lobby, you will see it furnished in red velvet, with oak appointments and brass chandeliers, just as Star and Bullock intended. Although

Bullock Hotel, Deadwood, Alan Leftridge

the building looks much the same as it did in 1900, it has had several upgrades and renovations, including the addition of a casino.

Some people claim that the hotel is haunted. Ask any staff member about their favorite story.

Look for advertising painted on the south side of the hotel, remnants of advertising for the Star and Bullock Store.

Mount Moriah Cemetery, Chad Coppess, South Dakota Tourism

3. Mount Moriah Cemetery

Many Old West towns have "Boot Hill" cemeteries where, it is said, gunfighters are buried who died with their boots on. In this cemetery, you will find the grave of one of the most famous people who died that way: Wild Bill Hickok. He is accompanied by 3,626 other people, and some are colorful characters of American lore. Next to Wild Bill is Calamity Jane. Other notable residents are Potato Creek Johnny, Preacher Smith, Vinegar Bill, and Seth Bullock. When you visit the cemetery, you'll see that it is divided into sections: Chinese, Jewish, Masonic, Civil War veterans, and "potter's field" for the indigents and prostitutes. Other graves scattered about the cemetery include children and a mass grave from a mine disaster. Established in the late 1870s, the historic Mount Moriah Cemetery no longer has spaces available. Individuals and families own the remaining plots.

4. Mount Theodore Roosevelt Monument

Seth Bullock erected this monument to honor his lifelong friend, Theodore Roosevelt. Chance brought the two together in 1884. Roosevelt, a deputy sheriff in Medora, North Dakota, was looking for a group of horse thieves when he and Bullock, the sheriff of Deadwood, happened to meet near Belle Fourche. The two became immediate friends. The 31-foot tower was dedicated July 4, 1919, seven months after Roosevelt's death. This was the first monument in the United States to honor the country's 26th president.

Mount Theodore Roosevelt Monument, Scott Bierly, Black Hills National Forest

Hotel Alex Johnson, Rapid City, Alan Leftridge

5. Hotel Alex Johnson

Completed in 1928 in downtown Rapid City, the Hotel Alex Johnson is listed on the National Register of Historic Places. The hotel is central in Alfred Hitchcock's Black Hills motion picture epic, *North by Northwest.* Cary Grant and Eva Marie Saint, the lead actors in the movie, stayed here, and also six U.S. presidents: Calvin Coolidge, Franklin Roosevelt, Dwight Eisenhower, Richard Nixon, Gerald Ford, and Ronald Reagan.

The Germanic Tudor exterior architecture transitions to a Plains Indian theme inside. Enter the lobby to be impressed by grand chandeliers and myriad wood carvings. The hotel retains the ambience of the late 1920s with original Native American art. Throughout the building you will discover photographs and newspaper clippings on display that chronicle the history of the hotel and Rapid City.

Many old hotels are said to be haunted. The Hotel Alex Johnson is no exception. The employees and guests keep a logbook of mysterious happenings. Alex Johnson, himself, is reported to be haunting the hotel since his death in 1938—supposedly to ensure the operations are run smoothly.

6. Mount Coolidge Lookout

A fire lookout tower was built atop 6,023-foot Mount Coolidge because of the summit's breathtaking 360-degree views. The Civilian Conservation Corps constructed this imposing building of local stone in the late 1930s. From the tower you can see Mount Rushmore, the Crazy Horse Memorial, the Needles, and, on a clear day, the Badlands, 60 miles east. Kiosk displays at the base of the tower interpret the 1988 Galena fire that burned 17,000 acres.

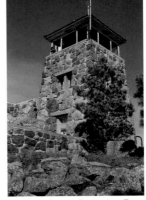

Mount Coolidge Fire Lookout Tower, Dick Kettlewell

7. Wildlife Station Visitor Center

The Civilian Conservation Corps constructed this beautiful building in the 1930s as the residence of the buffalo herdsman. Other park staff employees also occupied the house until 1990 when Custer State Park converted it into a visitor center. Its location along the southeast part of Wildlife Loop Road makes it a must-stop for touring if you are entering the

Wildlife Station Visitor Center, Dick Kettlewell

Black Hills from Hot Springs. Staff members provide information on wildlife and their habitats, and will help you plan your journey. The building's interior showcases the heralded artistry of the CCC craftsmen, featuring a bookstore and interpretive exhibits on wildlife and Custer State Park habitats.

Peter Norbeck Outdoor Education Center, Alan Leftridge

8. Peter Norbeck
Outdoor Education Center

The building is named to honor the South Dakota governor who is called the "Father of Custer State Park." Peter Norbeck championed the idea until the park was established in 1919. The Civilian Conservation Corps constructed the building in the 1930s. The architecture is fabulous. Here tourists can get information from park personnel, view exhibits about Custer State Park and the Black Hills, and shop at the bookstore. The Peter Norbeck Outdoor Education Center is a destination well worth touring.

Rock climbing on needles, Chad Coppess, South Dakota Tourism

BEST ICONIC PLACES

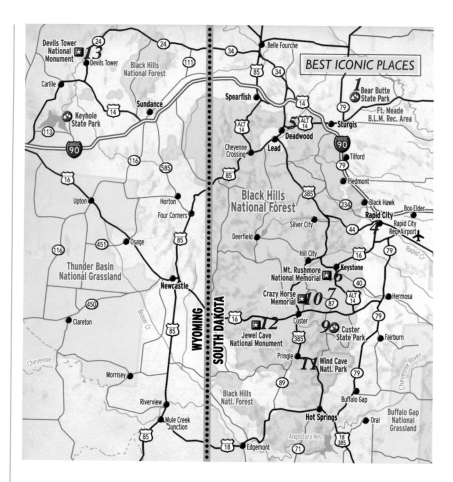

1. Bear Butte State Park

Called Bear Mountain by the Lakota and The Good Mountain by the Cheyenne, Bear Butte has drawn generations of sojourners to offer prayers and draw strength from the spirit of this mountain. Artifacts found in the vicinity reveal 10,000 years of Native American occupation.

Bear Butte, Alan Leftridge

Crazy Horse, Red Cloud, and Sitting Bull made pilgrimages to Bear

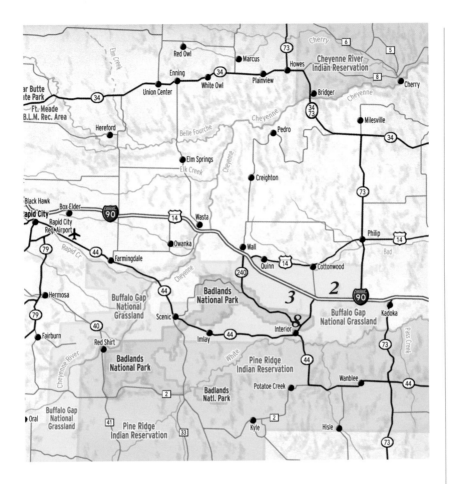

Butte. Today, native people visit the mountain to worship and leave offerings to their Creator. You will see these colorful prayer cloths and small pouches containing objects tied to trees.

Protected in Bear Butte State Park, the geologic feature is not technically a butte. The mountain formed in the same manner as Devils Tower. Lava intruded toward the surface through sedimentary layers 65 million years ago. The lava cooled to volcanic rock before breaking the surface. Thousands of years of rain and wind eroded the soft sedimentary rocks, leaving behind the harder volcanic rock of the mountain.

Visit the Bear Butte Lodge and Education Center at the base of the mountain to learn about tribal peoples' connections to the area and how the mountain got its names. Across the parking lot from the education center is the trailhead to the 1,250-foot summit. A hike to the top offers expansive views of the park's surroundings. Scan the immediate area to locate the small bison herd that roams here.

An easier hike takes you around Bear Butte Lake, a 215-acre reservoir west of Bear Butte. It offers great views of the lake with the mountain reflected in the water.

Bear Butte is a National Historic Landmark, honoring its significance as a religious place to Plains Indian tribes.

2. Minuteman Missile National Historic Site

Beginning in the early 1960s, the U.S. government deployed 1,000 Minuteman missiles on the prairies of Wyoming, Montana, North Dakota, and South Dakota. International treaties during the end of the Cold War led to decommis-

Minuteman Missile National Historic Site, Alan Leftridge

sioning 550 missiles and most of the sites (about 450 armed missiles remain siloed on the High Plains). Today, you can visit a Launch Control Facility that housed two Air Force officers and one decommissioned missile silo.

You can see a Minuteman Intercontinental Ballistic Missile in its silo. The bomb that was in its warhead was 1.2 megatons. It had seventy-five times greater yield—destructive power—than the atomic bomb dropped on Hiroshima in World War II. As you view the missile, consider that it could have unleashed the most destructive power that humans had ever created. How would you feel being one of the two launch officers in the Launch Control Center?

The visitor center is at Exit 131 on I-90, 75 miles east of Rapid City. The center has exhibits and information, including how to locate the Launch Control Facility and missile silo. Call for guided tour times and reservations.

3. Buffalo Gap National Grassland

You will be traveling through or next to Buffalo Gap National Grassland as you drive between Wall and Kadoka, South Dakota, on I-90. In

Prairie landscape, Chad Coppess, South Dakota Tourism

fact, the grassland surrounds Badlands National Park and the Minuteman Missile National Historic Site.

At nearly 600,000 acres, Buffalo Gap National Grassland is the second-largest grassland after the Little Missouri National Grassland in North Dakota. Buffalo Gap is one of twenty national grasslands that protect mixed-grass and tallgrass prairie ecosystems.

For a scenic 162-mile loop, drive east from Rapid City on I-90 to Exit 110 at Wall. Take SD 240 south through Buffalo Gap National Grassland and then east through Badlands National Park to SD 377. Turn south to SD 44 at Interior and follow it west through the grassland back to Rapid City.

Be sure to stop at the National Grasslands Visitor Center in Wall. Here you will find displays, an exhibit hall, theater, bookstore, and information about ways to experience the prairie firsthand. The center also offers checklists on prairie plants, grasses and forbs, and birds.

Bring your binoculars. There are many things to observe in this seemingly sedate prairie. Look for black-tailed prairie dogs, burrowing owls, foxes, pronghorn, and deer. Raptors hunt from above, and meadowlarks will serenade you along the route.

4. Rapid City

Every city has a heart, and Rapid City's is Main Street Square. The central feature of the square is its plaza where dozens of special events, concerts, and festivals occur throughout the year.

From Main Street Square, stroll the center of Rapid City's

Rapid City, Karlee Moore

culture and history. The downtown historic neighborhood bordered by Main, St. Joseph, 4th, and 9th Streets is packed with Native American arts and crafts, custom boutiques, quaint restaurants, art galleries, specialty shops, and early twentieth-century architecture. Be sure to visit the Hotel Alex Johnson on 6th Street. The interior is unique and beautiful.

U.S. president statues, Rapid City, Chad Coppess, South Dakota Tourism

Have your photo taken with a U.S. president! See how you measure up to your favorite. Every street corner has a life-size bronze statue of one of the past forty-three U.S. presidents.

While you are in Rapid City, visit the Journey Museum and Learning Center. This jewel, housed in a gorgeous modern building, is packed with exhibits and displays presenting the geography and human events that have shaped the Black Hills region. The Journey Museum is adjacent to the historic district at 222 New York Street, open daily, year-round.

Get the most of your time exploring the historic district by riding the City View Trolley or taking a walking tour. The Rapid City Convention & Visitors Center (444 Mount Rushmore Road) near the Journey Museum has current information on tours, including the City View Trolley, Downtown Rapid City Walking Tour, and a map to locate the statue of your favorite president.

5. Deadwood

Lieutenant Colonel George Armstrong Custer led an expedition of 1,000 soldiers and civilians through the Black Hills in the summer of 1874. They found traces of gold, and the news vaulted coast to coast. The Black Hills were within the Sioux Reservation and off-limits to white people. But with no resistance, prospectors, adventurers, gamblers, and business speculators overran the Black Hills. Between 1874 and 1877, at least 20,000 people illegally flooded the region. More than 3,000 residents were in Deadwood in 1876, the year that Wild Bill Hickok, Calamity Jane, and Seth Bullock arrived.

The mining camp had no government in the early days and consisted of tents and makeshift wooden structures scattered along sodden lanes covered in filth. The camp, cut out of a ponderosa pine forest, faced constant fire danger. The inevitable occurred on September 26, 1879, when an inferno torched most of the disheveled town. By then, however, Deadwood was on its way to permanence, and fire-resistant brick and stone buildings started to replace the shoddy wooden structures.

Deadwood, Alan Leftridge

Consolidated mining corporations soon bought out most prospectors' claims and big businesses stabilized the town's economy. As you tour Deadwood, look for the construction dates on buildings. Many of these buildings were constructed in the late 1800s and early 1900s, well after the rough-and-tumble Deadwood romanticized in motion pictures. The era of the quick-draw gunfighter and the hardscrabble prospector ended by 1930.

Today, Deadwood's allure remains in its sentimental connection to Wild West mythology, where grit, hard work, ingenuity, and independence paid off, and when conflicts were sometimes settled by who drew the fastest gun. The myth is kept alive today with the city's casinos, actors re-creating gunfights on Main Street, and a reenactment of Jack McCall's "miner's court" trial. Many businesses sport an Old West motif, with vintage photographs reminding people of the Black Hills legends and lore, and Deadwood's place in Americana.

The best time to see Deadwood is in the early morning before tourists crowd the sidewalks and vehicles pack the roads. Walk the quiet streets and enjoy the century-old Western architecture. Explore the main floor of the Bullock Hotel for a sense of early-day opulence, tour the Adams Museum for an accurate narrative of Deadwood's heyday, and walk the Mount Moriah Cemetery where Wild Bill, Calamity Jane, Potato Creek Johnny, and Seth Bullock are buried. Finally, go on a "treasure hunt" on Main Street and try to figure out where the "real" No. 10 Saloon was located.

6. Mount Rushmore National Memorial

Whose idea was it to carve Mount Rushmore for a national memorial?

Mount Rushmore National Memorial, Alan Leftridge

South Dakota state historian Doane Robinson began promoting the idea in 1923. Believing that "Tourists soon get fed up on scenery unless it has something of special interest connected with it to make it impressive," Robinson sought sculptors to carve the Needles. His vision was for several of the granite pillars to represent both Native Americans and pioneers. He proposed the project to Gutzon Borglum, and Borglum convinced him that he could carve a national memorial on Mount Rushmore rather than the Needles. Borglum championed a colossal sculpture of four presidents from their waists to foreheads: Washington represented the birth of America; Jefferson represented Western expansion; Lincoln, preserving the republic; and Teddy Roosevelt, the development of our country. After several years of negotiations among politicians, Borglum, and private parties, the carving began on October 4, 1927.

MOUNT RUSHMORE NATIONAL MEMORIAL

- *Annual visitation exceeds 3 million.*
- *The monument is granite which erodes at 1 inch every 10,000 years.*
- *The National Park Service took responsibility for the project in 1933.*
- *The cost of the project when stopped in 1941 was $989,992.*
- *Washington's face was finished in 1934.*
- *Jefferson was dedicated in 1936.*
- *Lincoln was completed in 1937.*
- *Roosevelt was dedicated in 1939.*
- *Originally Jefferson's head was to the left of Washington's, as you view the mountain. The rock was unsuited for carving and was blasted away, leaving the scar seen today.*
- *Each face is about 60 feet from chin to forehead.*
- *The original plans were for waist-high likenesses that would have made the monument 465 feet tall.*

Whether traveling east or west along SD 244, road signs indicate when you are nearing the memorial. Watch for a spectacular view of the sculpture 2.5 miles west of Keystone on SD 244. Also, as you travel along SD 244, prepare for a close-up view of Washington's profile to the north, about 2 miles after passing Horsethief Lake. These may be your very first glimpses of the carving. Of course, the best views are from within the national memorial itself.

You will likely spend at least 90 minutes here. The memorial is crowded from June to September. Plan to arrive before 10 A.M. or after 3 P.M. Visitation wanes during the winter months and the memorial is less crowded.

Mount Rushmore National Memorial is more than a massive sculpture. It is an iconic symbol of the principles of American democracy. It is yours to experience.

7. Black Hills Playhouse

Visit South Dakota's oldest summer theater. Sheltered in a ponderosa pine forest between the Needles Highway and Iron Mountain Road, the Black Hills Playhouse has advanced the fine arts and produced professional entertainment since 1946.

Black Hills Playhouse, Alan Leftridge

The vision of founder Dr. Warren M. "Doc" Lee was a summer stock theater offering University of South Dakota students, professors, and theater professionals an opportunity to develop and hone their talents and skills.

But where to locate? South Dakota was not a very populated state. Because the Black Hills area tourist traffic was heavy in summer, they began looking there. Custer State Park offered an old Civilian Conservation Corps camp, constructed in 1934. During the first summer season, the actors spent most days touring. In the second season, they performed in a tent theater. The CCC camp became home, and one of the permanent buildings served as a theater. Interest and attendance grew so much that, in 1955, the Game, Fish and Parks Commission provided the construction for a new theater, the one you visit today.

Feeling that the Black Hills Playhouse should include a play unique to the Black Hills area, the theater's founder, Dr. Warren "Doc" Lee, wrote in 1948 what is described as "historical fantasy," The Legend of Devil's Gulch. This popular standard ran for thirty-two years and was based on historical accounts of forgotten people who made small but significant contributions to the legacy of the Black Hills. Tourist audiences were delighted to experience stories about the colorful yet difficult times of the gold rush. The play evolved over time, adding characters, music, and lyrics. The Legend of Devil's Gulch exemplified the community spirit of the playhouse. Everyone in the company had the opportunity to work on the show in some way; even the smallest camp children would make their stage debuts in walk-on roles. If you are lucky, you may see a reprisal, here or in other South Dakota community theaters.

Musicals, dramas, and comedy are presented each summer from early June to late August. "End the Day with a Play," as Margaret "Wifie" Lee encouraged in her slogan from the fifties. Attending a performance in this gorgeous setting will be a delightful and memorable finale to your day of touring the park. It is as appealing today as ever.

Badlands National Park, Alan Leftridge

8. Badlands National Park

The eastern boundary of the Black Hills region is Badlands National Park. You can explore this geologic marvel by vehicle, on foot, and on horseback, and you will experience a landscape that changes every time it rains. This eroded landscape has some of the richest mammalian fossil beds in North America.

What do the skeletons of ancient camels, rhinoceroses, horses, and saber-toothed cats have in common? They are all found here. The badlands topography is geologically young. Successive volcanic flows and sediment deposits from a shallow sea overran this region about 75 million years ago. When the sea retreated, ancestral rivers snaked over the surface. Buried in the volcanic ash and sediments are a potpourri of mammalian fossil beds. Dinosaur fossils do not exist here. Remnants of long-extinct

BADLANDS NATIONAL PARK

- The park encompasses 244,000 acres.
- The name badland comes from the Lakota words mako sica, meaning "land bad."
- Badlands National Monument was established in 1939 and designated as a national park in 1978.
- The park is open year-round; visitor center hours and services vary with the season. Contact the park for updated information before your visit.
- An annual Badlands Astronomy Festival is scheduled every summer.

creatures are found near the surface because the ash and sediment deposits are soft and easily eroded by rain and wind. You can observe paleontologists excavating fossil remains at the Big Pig Dig event during summer.

Today, Badlands National Park's landscape of mixed-grass prairie is home to a wide variety of mammals. You might see bison, pronghorn, black-tailed prairie dogs, snakes, and if you are lucky, elusive black-footed ferrets.

Use Exit 110 or 131 along I-90 east of Rapid City onto SD 240 for a loop drive. The two-lane highway has several scenic overlooks of this otherworldly, awe-inspiring, and beautiful landscape.

Stretch your legs and learn more about the badlands by walking the accessible Fossil Exhibit Trail (a 0.5-mile round trip), the moderate Cliff Shelf loop trail (0.75 mile), and the Saddle Pass Trail for a view of the White River Valley (0.5 mile round trip). Make sure to visit Ben Reifel Visitor Center along the loop for an orientation film, updated information, interpretive exhibits, and a bookstore. Ask about the Big Pig Dig. Visitor center staff will direct you to the best photography spots and where to experience magnificent sunrises and sunsets. Watching a sunset is a wonderful way to finish the day, but don't leave yet. Night sky viewing in Badlands National Park is some of the best in North America!

9. Custer State Park

South Dakota's oldest and largest state park is here in the Black Hills. Custer State Park has more than 110 square miles of mountains, forests, prairies, streams, and lakes connected by a network of scenic roadways that crisscross the mountainous terrain. Keep your road map close—don't rely solely on GPS to help you navigate.

The geologically unparalleled Needles Highway and the Wildlife Loop Road are two scenic drives for you to explore. Stop at the Custer State

CUSTER STATE PARK

- *Founded in 1919, Custer was South Dakota's first state park.*
- *It is the largest South Dakota state park at 71,000 acres.*
- *The park is managed by South Dakota Game, Fish & Parks.*
- *The entrance fee varies depending on vehicle type.*
- *A herd of 1,300 bison roams throughout the park.*
- *An annual bison roundup is held the last Friday in September.*
- *Three scenic drives cross the park: Iron Mountain Road, Wildlife Loop Road, and the Needles Highway.*
- *President Calvin Coolidge made the State Game Lodge his "summer White House" in 1927.*
- *Members of Lt. Col. George Armstrong Custer's 1874 expedition to the Black Hills found traces of gold in the French Creek drainage.*

Park Visitor Center, Peter Norbeck Visitor Center, or the Wildlife Station Visitor Center to get the current conditions and learn more about the park before you set out.

Prized for its watchable wildlife, the park has a free-roaming bison herd of 1,300. Look for bison alongside and sometimes crossing the road. Lone bulls lounge on distant hillsides. Other wildlife that you might see are pronghorn, mountain goats, bighorn sheep, mule deer, elk, and wild turkeys. Not so wild are the feral burros that stop traffic and beg for attention along the Wildlife Loop Road.

Spring through autumn brings a profusion of floral color to Custer State Park. Swaths of wildflowers adorn the roadsides and embellish the hills. Forest floors are spangled in seasonal colors. Look for black-eyed Susan, blue flax, wild rose, and paintbrush along the roads. The hills and prairies are covered in sticky geranium, coneflowers, and arrowleaf balsamroot, while the forest floors present oxalis, calypso orchids, and monkeyflowers. You will find harebells and yarrow flowers in every possible location.

Sylvan Lake in Custer State Park,
Beth Steinhauer, Black Hills National Forest

BEGGING BURROS

Christopher Columbus brought the ancestors of today's burros to the Western Hemisphere on his second voyage. Their offspring found their way to the West as pack animals during the gold rush era. Many escaped or were released into the wild when they were no longer needed. In the Black Hills,

Begging burros, Chad Coppess, South Dakota Tourism

they carried tourists up Black Elk Peak during the last century. Burros were released into the park when the tours were discontinued. Free to roam in Custer State Park, they became naturalized to the environment.

Park managers recognize them as feral rather than wild and place no restrictions on visitors for feeding them. Like many animals acclimated to being around humans, these charismatic relatives of the horse readily accept food handouts. About four dozen burros inhabit a hilly area of the Wildlife Loop Road, where they garner attention from passing motorists. Walking onto the road to impede traffic, they move close to vehicles and panhandle for food, giving them the moniker "begging burros."

Cute and lovable as they appear, some are bold. They will stick their noses through an open window to demand a handout. They may not seem dangerous, but they can bite and have been known to even snack on vehicle door handles and side-view mirrors.

Consider the many options if you plan on spending the night in Custer State Park. Campgrounds are abundant, ten in all. Select from a lakeside site or near a lodge. If indoor accommodations are your preference, the park has contemporary and rustic overnight resorts at Sylvan Lake, Legion Lake, Blue Bell, and the State Game Lodge.

The park is also rich in family recreational opportunities: historic sites, visitor centers, fishing lakes, safaris, horseback rides, hayrides, and interpretive programs. Adventure beckons via the miles of trails and backcountry roads to explore on mountain bikes, on horseback, and on foot.

BUFFALO ROUNDUP

Within the 71,000-acre Custer State Park is one of the largest publicly owned bison herds in the world. And because of that, you are pretty much guaranteed to see bison whenever you visit.

The three best times to observe bison are during their courtship rut in August, calving season in May, and the last Friday in September,

Buffalo Roundup, Custer State Park, Chad Coppess, South Dakota Tourism

when Custer State Park personnel conduct the annual Buffalo Roundup.

The park's prairies can sustain about 1,300 bison, so each year hundreds of excess animals are culled during the roundup to be relocated to other managed areas, or sold at auction. The event is a spectacle that more than 10,000 people attend to watch real cowboys and cowgirls bring in the thundering herd.

The Buffalo Roundup gives a sense of the Old West. As you feel the rumble beneath your feet, you can visualize the time when thousands of bison would stampede across the prairie thorough clouds of flying dust. See www.gfp.sd.gov for information about the upcoming roundup.

10. Crazy Horse Memorial

Many Native Americans were insulted by the creation of Mount Rushmore National Memorial. It was built on sacred ground to many and celebrated Western expansion that appropriated their homelands.

To offset the faces on Rushmore, Lakota Chief Henry Standing Bear imagined a carving that would honor a great Indian leader. In 1939, he invited sculptor Korczak Ziolkowski to create a memorial in the Black Hills to a great Native American leader. Ziolkowski eventually agreed to the idea and, with Standing Bear, made a plan for the monument. They selected a granite-ridged mountaintop near Mount Rushmore for the

Crazy Horse Memorial, Alan Leftridge

CRAZY HORSE MEMORIAL

- More than 1 million people a year visit the memorial.
- The project is funded by admission fees and contributions.
- Crazy Horse's face was completed and dedicated in 1998.
- When complete, the entire carving will be 563 feet high and 641 feet long.

sculpture. The mountain is considered Lakota property and is sacred. Recognizing that Gutzon Borglum (the sculptor for Mount Rushmore) struggled with funding and oversight issues because he relied on government money, Ziolkowski determined to finance the project with private funds.

The freestanding statue is of the great Oglala Lakota warrior Crazy Horse. His exemplary character, leadership, loyalty, and will to preserve the culture of his people made him an ideal choice even though there is no authenticated photograph of his likeness.

A dynamite blast inaugurated the carving in 1948. It is larger than any of the figures on Mount Rushmore. Korczak Ziolkowski sculpted the mountain for thirty-four years until his death in 1982. Among his last requests to his wife was: "You must work on the mountain, but go slowly so you do it right." His family has continued carving the mountain since his death, but the completion date is unknown.

Crazy Horse points east as he proclaims, "My land is where my dead lie buried," affirming perpetual Indian ownership of the Black Hills region.

In Ziolkowski's working model, Crazy Horse is pointing with his index finger, which has sparked a controversy. In 1926, the elder brother of Chief Henry Standing Bear, Luther Standing Bear, wrote, "When the scout pointed he used his thumb instead of the first finger." Many cultures judge finger pointing as rude behavior. It remains to be seen how the Ziolkowski family will carve the great warrior's outstretched arm.

11. Wind Cave National Park

Air moves into and out of caves, equalizing the atmospheric pressure between the inner and outer worlds. When the air pressure is higher outside, air flows into the

Wind Cave NP, NPS photo

83

WIND CAVE NATIONAL PARK

- First national park in the world to protect a cave.
- Established as the seventh national park in 1903.
- Third-longest cave in the United States.
- Sixth-longest cave in the world, with more than 143 miles of passages.

Wind Cave NP, Alan Leftridge

- Its great volume makes it the fourth-largest cave on Earth.
- The cave is within a 1.1- by 1.3-mile rectangle.
- Mean cave temperature is 53 degrees F.
- The surface area of the park is 33,851 acres, or 44 square miles.

caves. When the air pressure outside is lower, air flows out of the caves. The air movement is negligible for caves with large openings, but caves with small openings can produce noticeable winds.

The natural entrance of Wind Cave is small for a large cave. The cave's volume, however, is huge. At 39 million cubic feet, it is 2 million cubic feet larger than the Empire State Building. The cave gets its name from the rushing air that equalizes pressure through a small opening. The highest wind speed measured at the original entrance is 25 miles per hour!

European settlers assigned the name, yet the Sioux people were well aware of the cave for hundreds of years. They consider the opening a sacred place, the source of their people's origination.

Wind Cave National Park houses one of the longest caves in the world. Spelunkers continue to explore the cave, mapping areas no humans have been before. Wind Cave has few stalactites and stalagmites but many unique mineral formations. You too can experience this underground world with a guided tour. The 60-minute Garden of Eden Cave Tour is the shortest and easiest option. A park interpreter will point out several of the cave's unusual formations. A longer and more strenuous tour is the Natural Entrance Cave Tour. This 90-minute experience takes you to the spot where the cave was discovered and will introduce you to the world's largest display of boxwork, a rare honeycomb-like calcite formation.

Spend ample time in the visitor center while awaiting your tour.

Exhibits cover cave exploration, cave formations, early cave history, local Civilian Conservation Corps projects, and information about the park.

Aboveground, the park encompasses 33,851 acres of mixed-grass prairies and ponderosa pine forests. The land is home to elk, pronghorn, mule deer, black-tailed prairie dogs, and over 450 bison.

After a long drive or a cave tour, stretch your legs on a hike and watch for some of the iconic fauna of Wind Cave National Park. Inquire at the visitor center and choose a hike from more than 30 miles of park trails. Consider Wind Cave Canyon Trail, an easy 1.8-mile walk along a closed road to the edge of the park to view beautiful limestone cliffs. Another easy hike is Rankin Ridge Interpretive Trail. The 1-mile walk offers great views from the park's highest point. The 1.4-mile Cold Brook Canyon Trail requires moderate exertion. It drops into a canyon, then winds west toward the park boundary. Watch for raptors and other birds along the cliffs.

As you leave the park, look for the small colony of prairie dogs at the main entrance. They are active, easy to see, and fun to watch.

12. Jewel Cave National Monument

Discover one of the last frontiers! You will only be able to explore a small part of the cave during your tour because Jewel Cave is huge. The mapped and surveyed passages of Jewel Cave account for 182 miles, making it the third-longest cave

Jewel Cave, Chad Coppess, South Dakota Tourism

in the world. Researchers estimate that the surveyed area is only about 3 percent of the overall cave volume. How did this cave get so massive?

The cave system continues to form as gravity forces groundwater downward through small cracks in the limestone layers. The mildly acidic water slowly dissolves the rock. Dissolved limestone also is acidic. As the now acid-rich water disintegrates more of the stone, the cracks enlarge. The process began 60 million years ago at the time of the Black Hills uplift, and Jewel Cave continues its slow growth today. Surveying and mapping is ongoing as explorers find new passages. No one knows where Jewel Cave ends.

JEWEL CAVE

- *Jewel Cave National Monument is open year-round.*
- *World's third-longest cave with over 182 miles surveyed.*
- *Named after calcite spar crystal clusters on the walls.*
- *Monument encompasses 1,273 acres aboveground.*
- *President Theodore Roosevelt established the monument on February 1, 1908.*
- *The National Park Service began managing the monument in 1933 and began offering tours in 1939.*

Visit Jewel Cave on a guided tour. On the 1.5-hour Scenic Tour, you will see clusters of jewel-like calcite spar crystals that give the cave its name. Other geologic features for which the cave is famed include gypsum flowers, needles, spiders, and rare hydromagnesite balloons. Have a more intimate experience with the cave by going on a 1.75-hour Historic Lantern Tour or a strenuous 3- to 4-hour Wild Caving Tour (reservations are required).

There is more to Jewel Cave National Monument than the cave. The aboveground monument encompasses 1,273 acres. Here the mixed-grass prairie ecosystem of plants and animals meets the fauna and flora of the Rocky Mountains. Explore three trails that access the overlapping ecosystems. Maps at the visitor center will help you find the trailheads; be sure to ask about current trail conditions and what you might discover on your hike.

A limited number of visitors can participate in each guided cave tour. You may need to wait. If so, consider stretching your legs on the A Walk on the Roof Trail. This 30-minute, 0.25-mile loop begins at the covered patio and returns to the visitor center. Imagine the cave below your feet as you walk through the ponderosa pine forest. Look for interpretive signs that explain how the cave and the topside surface interrelate.

13. Devils Tower National Monument

Your first glimpse of Devils Tower is from afar. Your awe grows the closer you approach. Devils Tower is truly a unique geological feature, and it's easy to appreciate why it was selected to be the first national monument.

You are not alone in your admiration of the tower. Oral tradition tells that Native Americans long ago honored it with respect and placed it as the center of some of their creation stories. Some Indians referred to it as Bear Lodge, Bear's Tipi, and Great Gray Horn. Today, over twenty Plains Indian tribes consider Devils Tower to be a sacred site and hold their own names for the feature.

The official government name today is Devils Tower. The name comes from an 1875 U.S. Geological Survey expedition into the Black Hills led by Colonel Richard Dodge. He wrote in his 1876 book, *The Black Hills*, that some of the Indians in the region called it in their language "the bad god's tower." That name was interpreted in English to be "devil's tower," and the name stuck.

Devils Tower, Alan Leftridge

Notice the tower's vertical rock columns. Interpreters with the National Park Service suggest that you think of the layers as bunched pencils held together by gravity. How did such an odd feature form?

Many tens of millions of years ago, shallow seas repeatedly covered western South Dakota, most of Wyoming, and eastern Montana. When the last of the seas receded, what remained were countless layers of sedimentary limestone and sandstone.

About 60 million years ago, volcanic activity began to uplift the entire region. Molten rock (magma) upwelled in many areas but never broke the surface to cause a volcanic flow. Instead, the surface rose, and the central bulge became today's Black Hills. At this spot, the magma found cracks in the sedimentary

DEVILS TOWER

- Devils Tower is 867 feet tall from its base to the summit.
- The circumference of the base of the tower is 1 mile.
- The top is about the size of a football field.
- The summit is slightly dome shaped and rocky, with native grasses, cacti, and sagebrush. Chipmunks, mice, pack rats, and the occasional snake are found on top.

overlying rocks and was pushed vertically toward the surface. The igneous intrusion stopped before breaking through the top and cooling. Millions of years of erosion from sources like the present-day Little Missouri River and the Belle Fourche River washed away the softer sedimentary layers leaving the more resistant volcanic rocks of the Devils Tower.

Those vertical rock layers are similar to granite and known as phonolite porphyry. The chemical composition of the stone caused the hot molecules to align in long crystal-like arrangements as the magma cooled.

So what's on top? Thousands of people have made it there, all by climbing, except one person who parachuted, after which he was stranded for several days, requiring a rescue. Today, parachuting to the top is not allowed. What did he, and others who have climbed to the top, find? The summit plain is about the size of a football field, with plants and smaller animals that are also found around the tower. Sagebrush, grasses, and cacti help support mice, chipmunks, and a few of their predators like snakes and raptors. The summit also offers an unparalleled panoramic view of the vast prairie below.

Gain deeper appreciation of Devils Tower by stopping at the visitor center at the end of Route 110 in the monument. Ask questions of the National Park Service personnel and peruse the bookstore. I recommend two hikes: Tower Trail of 1.3 miles that circumnavigates the tower, and Joyner Ridge Trail, a 1.5-mile walk that gives fantastic views north of Devils Tower.

TRIBAL SITES

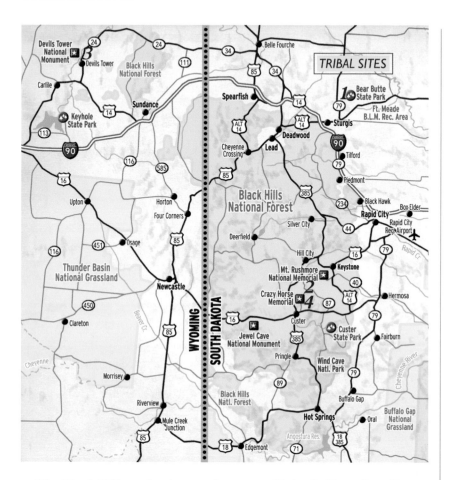

The Black Hills region is sacred to many Plains Indian tribes. Ponca, Arapaho, Kiowa, Cheyenne, Crow, and Lakota people have a long and sustained history of spiritual connection here. Rather than using churches or other buildings, native people find special places for spiritual ceremonies and growth in nature.

When you visit sacred sites, you may see colorful pieces of cloth and small bundles hanging from trees. These are prayer cloths and tobacco ties that signify prayers offered here by individuals during their worship. Please respect these, leaving them undisturbed.

1. Bear Butte

People from many Native American tribes come here to hold sacred ceremonies. Many native people believe that Bear Butte is the place where the creator has chosen to communicate with them through divinations.

2. Black Elk Peak

Called *Hinhan Kaga* by the Lakota, this is where their revered medicine man, Black Elk, received his vision at the age of nine. Describing his vision, he said, "And while I stood there I saw more than I can tell and I understood more than I saw; for I was seeing in a sacred manner the shapes of all things in the spirit, and the shape of all shapes as they must live together like one being."

3. Devils Tower

Many native people consider the tower sacred. The Kiowa, Cheyenne, Crow, Shoshone, Arapaho, and Lakota tribes each have stories connecting people with the geologic feature. Some oral traditions relate strong connections of the tower to the night sky.

Crazy Horse Memorial, Gary Chancey, Black Hills National Forest

4. Crazy Horse Mountain

The Crazy Horse Memorial and the lands immediately around the carving are considered sacred by Oglala Lakota. The Crazy Horse Memorial is devoted to the great leaders of all Native Americans. When a cavalryman asked Crazy Horse, "Where are your lands, now?" he replied, "My lands are where my dead lie buried." The carving shows him pointing across the Black Hills toward the grasslands.

Spirituality is collective and also personal. The Black Hills are sacred to native tribes, while some individuals have their own special areas, unbeknownst to others, for worship, vision quests, hunting game, and gathering medicines.

Bear Butte, Alan Leftridge

BEST MAMMALS

The Black Hills region is rich in both native and non-native wildlife adapted to living in this diverse area of mountains, prairie, rivers, and lakes. Watchable wildlife you should expect to see include bison, pronghorn, elk, coyotes, prairie dogs, bighorn sheep, chipmunks, mountain goats, tree squirrels, deer, and burros. If you look carefully, you may encounter elusive flying squirrels, bats, marmots, beavers, and jackrabbits.

Although you will want to take photos, you might not have time to grab your camera. Many of these sightings may last only an instant. So enjoy these moments. Build your vacation memories by recording your discoveries on the checklist. Return to the Black Hills often so you can add reclusive mountain lions, badgers, foxes, and black-footed ferrets to your list.

Beaver
Castor canadensis

Can you imagine trying to build a stick-and-mud dam across a flowing stream, at night? That is what beavers do. They are engineers, reconstructing landscapes to make them suitable beaver habitat. Their resulting ponds

Beaver, NPS photo

encourage willows, a favored food, to grow along the shore. Beaver ponds attract other animals and provide habitat for the plants on which they depend. Over time, their ponds fill with silt and become meadows, serving as new homes for the Black Hills' elk, deer, porcupines, bobcats, and foxes.

Best Places to See Beavers
Beavers are found throughout South Dakota. They are most active in the morning and evening. Find a stream or pond with gnawed trees nearby. Look for a pile of branches and mud stopping the water flow. Sit and wait in an obscure location and you may soon see a beaver swimming by.

Yellow-bellied Marmot
Marmota flaviventris

A little larger than a football with a tail, yellow-bellied marmots are also known as rockchucks and whistle pigs. A ground squirrel by definition,

Yellow-bellied marmot, Alan Leftridge

they can weigh up to eleven pounds.

Living in colonies on rocky slopes, in meadows with boulders nearby, and along cliff faces in the Black Hills, these grizzled-looking rodents are recognized by their mock boxing matches, nuzzling of one another, conspicuous sunbathing, and standing on their hind legs chirping out whistles. They fatten themselves during the summer on grasses and flowers and burn off the fat in hibernation, which accounts for about 60 percent of their lives!

Best Places to Yellow-bellied Marmots

Look for yellow-bellied marmots at the Needles Eye and Black Elk Peak.

Black-tailed Prairie Dog
Cynomys ludovicianus

You will hear warning calls similar to small dogs barking as you walk toward a prairie dog town. While some prairie dogs forage, others are sentinels, watching for predators. Although you are not a hawk, coyote, snake, or black-footed ferret, the lookouts will react to your presence with a cautious cry.

Prairie dogs live in social groups as small as their core family and as large as a colony. Large underground colonies are

Black-tailed praire dog, Alan Leftridge

called "towns." The largest black-tailed prairie dog town may be one in western Texas that stretches 100 miles long.

Today, 10 to 20 million prairie dogs live in the mixed-grass prairies of the western states. That's just 5 percent of the population that existed before pioneers settled the West. Prairie dogs competed with cattle for grazing, and their burrows made plowing difficult. Prairie dogs were labeled pests and targeted for eradication.

Today, black-tailed prairie dog populations have increased in many places to the point that government land managers have reintroduced the prairie dog's most feared predator, the black-footed ferret. More than fifty ferrets now live in the prairie dog towns of Badlands National Park.

Best Places to See Black-tailed Prairie Dogs

Look for colonies of prairie dogs in Devils Tower National Monument, Wind Cave National Park, and Wildlife Loop Road, Custer State Park, and Badlands National Park.

Little brown bat, NPS photo

Little Brown Bat
Myotis lucifugus

Hold three nickels in your hand. That is about the weight of a little brown bat. Their small mass and several unique anatomical features allow them to be the only mammals capable of flight. Now look at your hand. The bat's wing anatomically resembles yours, having long finger bones that are connected by a membrane stretching between them.

Emerging from their roosts at twilight, brown bats patrol the night sky, devouring swarms of flying insects. Their favorites are wasps and moths. By dawn, each bat will have consumed insects equal to half its body weight.

Little brown bats are the most numerous bats in North America. They live about ten years if they are fortunate to avoid a fungal disease called white-nose syndrome during their four- to six-month hibernation period.

Best Places to See Little Brown Bats

Little brown bats find suitable living quarters in structures that we build. When you pass some of the older buildings in the Black Hills, you may hear them communicating with each other from within with clicks and squeaks. Look for them at sunset around Wind Cave and Jewel Cave.

Northern Flying Squirrel
Glaucomys sabrinus

As the sky begins to darken at the close of day, you might settle before a campfire. From the corner of your eye, you detect something gliding among the trees. While you are getting ready to sleep, many animals are awakening.

The glider may have been a northern flying squirrel. Contrary to their name, they cannot fly. Cape-like flaps of skin that stretch between their front and rear legs enable them to glide from one tree to the next. The squirrels climb a tree to a certain height and launch themselves toward a distant tree. They have a flight ratio of 3, meaning that they can soar 30 feet for every 10 feet of descent. People in hang gliders come close to this rate.

Northern flying squirrel, J. Schmidt, NPS photo

Northern flying squirrels live in the same forests as red squirrels and, like red squirrels, do not hibernate. They nestle with family members, staying cozy in abandoned woodpecker holes on cold days.

Best Places to See Northern Flying Squirrels

Because they are active at night, a good strategy for seeing northern flying squirrels is to camp at any campground with tall ponderosa pine or spruce trees. Look up as evening falls—you might see a flying squirrel!

Red squirrel, Mike Gue??, NPS photo

Red Squirrel
Tamiasciurus hudsonicus

These tree acrobats will amuse you with their charming antics as they pursue each other up and down tree trunks and leap from limb to limb. You may discover these squirrels by sight or from their ruckus. Their noisy chattering is a territorial call. With a home range of less than two football fields and population densities of two squirrels to three acres, their boundaries often overlap. They do not like to share their cached food and will battle to guard it. Red squirrels do not hibernate and can live ten years if they can stay away from owls, martens, foxes, and bobcats.

Best Places to See Red Squirrels

Red squirrels feed on pine and spruce cones, so look and listen for them in the spruce forest in Spearfish Canyon, and throughout the ponderosa forests of the Black Hills region.

Least Chipmunk
Tamias minimus

Few scenes are more charming than a chipmunk resting on a rock with forepaws folded against its chest.

These members of the squirrel family are in the genus Tamias, which is Greek for "storer." Chipmunks hoard food in underground caches for winter. Their periods of dormancy can last from many days to several weeks. They often awaken during winter and feed on their larder until hibernation ends in April.

Least chipmunk, Jacob W. Frank, NPS photo

Their diet consists of berries, nuts, fruit, flowers, conifer seeds, leaves, grasses, pollen, mushrooms, insects, and birds' eggs.

Chipmunks play a significant role in scattering seeds, thereby dispersing the plants. They spend much of their day hiding seeds in every possible spot. Seeds that they fail to retrieve often sprout.

Not by their choosing, chipmunks play a vital role as prey for many mammals and birds. If they avoid predators, they can live up to six years.

Best Places to See Least Chipmunks
These affable squirrels are common at Devils Tower National Monument and around most human dwellings in Custer State Park.

Bighorn sheep, Chad Coppess, South Dakota Tourism

Bighorn Sheep
Ovis canadensis

Whether on mountainsides or in meadows, bighorn sheep like to congregate—sometimes in groups of up to 100. Autumn is when the males compete for dominance, using their impressive, curved horns. The rams square off about 10 feet apart, rise up on their hind legs, tuck their chins, and lunge toward each other at over 20 miles per hour. The resulting crack of sound can be heard more than a mile away, carried on quiet Black Hills' air.

KEEP WILDLIFE WILD AND HEALTHY

Feeding wildlife may be entertaining, but it leads to problems. Animals become a nuisance around picnic areas and camp-grounds, and they sometimes carry diseases that can spread to humans. Our food is meant for people. It does not provide the nutrients that wildlife need to survive. Animals that become habituated to human food become malnourished and will not survive the stress of severe winters in the Black Hills.

Be careful with food. An open bag of garbage, an unattended bowl of pet food, or a lazily discarded plate of leftover picnic morsels can severely harm wildlife. Healthy wild animals have a natural fear of people and keep their distance. Wild animals that have access to your pet's food or your garbage can lose their fear and become aggressive. Wildlife managers reluctantly must use extreme measures to remove habituated animals.

For the sake of the wildlife, keep your picnic area and campsite clean and free of food attractants.

Best Places to See Bighorn Sheep

Not all bighorn sheep are on mountainsides or in meadows. They are often seen near the entrance to Custer State Park by the State Game Lodge.

Mountain Goat

Oreamnos americanus

People sometimes confuse mountain goats and bighorn sheep. Mountain goats have straight, sharp, black horns, a short tail, and an elongated face. Bighorn sheep horns are gray or brown and are deeply curled. Sheep are mostly gray to tan, while goats are white. You can also distinguish them by where they are found. Bighorn sheep live on rocky slopes

Mountain goat, Chad Coppess, South Dakota Tourism

with ample grass, while goats prefer higher, cliff-ridden mountain peaks and ridges.

Mountain goats spend most of their time grazing on grasses, herbs, ferns, mosses, and lichens. When not feeding, they rest on rocky cliffs protected from mountain lions. Sure-footed climbers at high elevations, their cloven hooves can spread apart, while their inner pads provide traction to help them navigate steep rocky slopes. They can live 15 years in the protected areas of the Black Hills region.

Best Places to See Mountain Goats

Mountain goats are non-native to the Black Hills. Six were introduced in the mid-1920s and they have flourished since. Look for mountain goats on Black Elk Peak, at Mount Rushmore National Memorial, and along the high cliffs in Spearfish Canyon.

Pronghorn, Wind Cave NP, NPS photo

Pronghorn
Antilocapra americana

North American pronghorn evolved in an ecological niche comparable to that of the African antelope. Both have similar behavior and needs.

They inhabit grasslands and are speedy. The two animals are so alike that many people refer to pronghorn as antelope. The pronghorn's closest living relatives, however, are giraffes.

Pronghorn are the world's greatest marathon land animals. Open prairie environments are critical for their survival. Their bone and muscular structure do not allow them to leap over obstructions like fences. They are adapted to places where they use speed to avoid predators. Pronghorn can bolt to 60 miles per hour and maintain half that rate for 6 or 7 miles. Even a week-old pronghorn can outrun any dog.

Best Places to See Pronghorn

Look for pronghorn in open spaces in Wind Cave National Park, Badlands National Park, along Wildlife Loop Road in Custer State Park, and along I-90 and SD 79.

Mule Deer

Odocoileus hemionus

Larger and darker colored than white-tailed deer, mule deer are recognized by their large "mule" ears, their short tail with black markings, and their bounding gait on all four legs as they escape trouble.

Like their cousins the white-tailed

Mule deer doe and fawn, Wind Cave NP, NPS photo

deer, mule deer are browsers. Where their habitats overlap, their diets vary enough that they do not directly compete for food.

Mule deer live up to 11 years in protected areas if, as adults, they avoid mountain lions, and, as fawns, are lucky to avoid coyotes, eagles, and bobcats.

Best Places to See Mule Deer

Watch for mule deer in Custer State Park, Wind Cave National Park, and Devils Tower National Monument.

White-tailed Deer

Odocoileus virginianus

Can you picture spending nearly half of your day eating? White-tailed deer pass more than 40 percent of their day browsing on grasses, brushy plants, twigs, and leaves. You will know white-tailed deer by their large white tails, which they flash as a warning when startled or frightened. When they must, they can escape at 30 miles per hour, bound as high as 10 feet, and bolt across a highway in one vault. White-tailed deer are common in the Black Hills and can survive 16 years if they avoid predators and vehicles.

White-tailed deer doe and fawn, Alan Leftridge

Best Places to See White-tailed Deer

Common places to find white-tailed deer are at Devils Tower National Monument, Jewel Cave National Monument, and Wildlife Loop Road in Custer State Park.

Rocky Mountain Elk

Cervus elaphus nelsoni

Much larger than either a mule deer or a white-tailed deer, elk are a majestic spectacle in the Black Hills' forests.

It is difficult to spot elk in the summer because they travel in small groups in the high country. Autumn is the best

Rocky Mountain elk, Wind Cave NP, NPS photo

season to see many elk, when they move to the lower elevations. This is when the bulls compete with one another as they collect their harems. In October, you may be lucky to hear the sound of the males bugling on a frosty morning to attract cows.

WATCHING WILDLIFE

Observe wildlife at a distance that does not change the animal's behavior. This is for your safety and to avoid disturbing the animal. It is illegal to willfully remain near or approach wildlife within any distance that disturbs or displaces the animal.

Consider every animal wild and possibly dangerous. Do not approach any animal. Bison may look lethargic, but even at a lazy-looking 2,000 pounds, they can lunge with surprising speed. It is the only member of the bovine family that does not close its eyes the instant before striking. It always hits its target.

Elk have been known to lower their heads and charge people they consider a danger; those lovable big-eyed deer will rear on their hind legs to strike with their sharp fore-hooves.

Mountain goats can become cantankerous and charge from short distance. You don't want to challenge those sharp horns.

Even small mammals are a concern. Feeding marmots and chipmunks by hand runs the risk of serious bites and contracting diseases.

Keep wildlife wild. Enjoy them at a safe distance.

Elk can live up to 14 years when protected in wild places. Older bulls in prime condition can grow antler racks wider than 8 feet across.

Best Places to See Rocky Mountain Elk

Both Wind Cave National Park and Custer State Park have populations of Rocky Mountain elk.

Bison

Bison bison

The American bison is the most emblematic animal of the Wild West. (You can find the bison profile on the National Park Service patch.) They evolved in Euro-Asia during the Pleistocene era and migrated to North America around 12,000

Bison, NPS photo

years ago, outlasting woolly mammoths to become the largest land animals on the continent. When European migrants arrived on eastern shores, an estimated 60 million bison roamed the grasslands and forests as far east as Pennsylvania; south to Florida's panhandle; across Louisiana,

HOW FAST CAN THEY RUN?

How would you match up in a race? The following are maximum speeds (in miles per hour, or mph) of the animals found in the Black Hills region. Some animals can sustain these speeds over long distances, while others represent sprints.

- Red squirrel 12 mph
- White-tailed deer 30 mph
- Bison 30 mph
- Black bear 33 mph
- Mule deer 35 mph
- Mountain lion 35 mph
- Snowshoe rabbit 38 mph
- Coyote 43 mph
- Elk 45 mph
- Pronghorn 53 mph
- Fastest Olympic sprinter 27 mph

If you were an Olympic sprinter, you could only outrun a red squirrel.

Texas, and northern Mexico; north to the plains of Saskatchewan and Alberta; and west to northern California. Almost hunted to extinction in the 1800s, today only about 15,000 bison roam in North America, and nearly 1,600 of those are in Custer State Park's 71,000 acres.

Bison can weigh up to half as much as your car. These seemingly passive animals are extremely powerful, quick, and unpredictable. Without warning, they can charge at up to 40 miles per hour.

Best Places to See Bison

Bison are found throughout Custer State Park, especially along Wildlife Loop Road. Look for bison in herds, small groups, and as single animals around Norbeck Visitor Center and the State Game Lodge. You may also see them at Sage Creek in Badlands National Park.

Coyote

Canis latrans

It usually starts with a single yelp in the night. In less than a minute, several more coyotes will join the chorus. Coyotes are numerous and dwell in every possible part of the Black Hills. They flourish because they

A CHECKLIST OF MAMMALS IN THE BLACK HILLS REGION

_____ Beaver		_____ Mule Deer	
_____ Bighorn Sheep		_____ Northern Flying Squirrel	
_____ Bison		_____ Pronghorn	
_____ Black-tailed Prairie Dog		_____ Red Squirrel	
_____ Coyote		_____ Rocky Mountain Elk	
_____ Least Chipmunk		_____ White-tailed Deer	
_____ Little Brown Bat		_____ Yellow-bellied Marmot	
_____ Mountain Goat			

adapt well to changing conditions, like deforestation and urbanization. Coyotes blend well with grasses and sagebrush, but you may spot one trotting down a road in front of your car. If you don't see a coyote, listen for its yelping as darkness falls.

Best Places to See Coyotes

Look for coyotes in the fields and meadows of Wind Cave National Park, Custer State Park, Devils Tower National Monument, and Badlands National Park.

Coyote, L. K. Duvanich

BEST PLACES TO SEE
WILDLIFE FROM THE ROAD

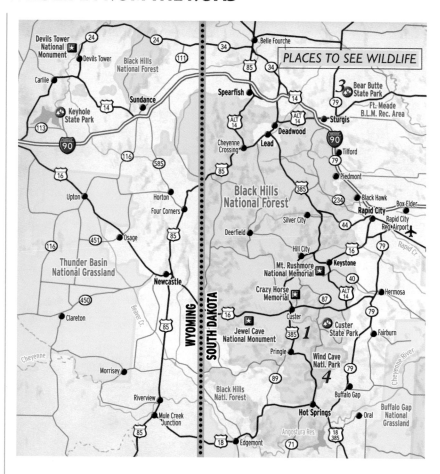

Wildlife abounds in the Black Hills region. Your watchful eye will likely catch a glimpse of wildlife anywhere, whether traveling the interstate, state highways, county roads, or backroads. Look for things that stand out in the landscape. They may be pronghorn, deer, bison, or raptors.

There are roads along which you are almost sure to see wildlife; here are a few:

1. Custer State Park, Wildlife Loop Road

You will see some of the 1,300 bison that live in the park. Pronghorn roam the hillsides in small groups. Black-tailed prairie dog towns are

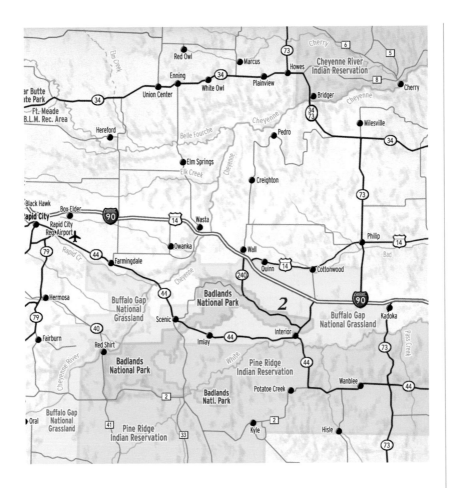

scattered alongside the road. Raptors such as red-tailed hawks and kestrels hunt above the prairie. You will hear songbirds singing from fence posts and tree snags.

2. Badlands National Park, SD Hwy 240

Pronghorn and black-tailed prairie dog towns are common along SD 240. Large groups of bison, black-tailed prairie dogs, and pronghorn live along Sage Creek Road.

3. Bear Butte State Park, Entrance Road

Watch for bison from the park entrance sign to the visitor center.

Bison, Chad Coppess, South Dakota Tourism

4. Wind Cave National Park, Entrance Road

Look for the colony of black-tailed prairie dogs near the park entrance.

Stop in the visitor centers and ask rangers for the latest information on animal sightings.

BEST BIRDS

More than 350 species of birds can be found in and around the Black Hills region. The wide diversity of habitats, from arid badlands, prairies, and waterways to mountain peaks, provides food and cover for songbirds, jays, waterfowl, upland birds, raptors, and more. Some birds can be seen as you drive the region's roads, but you'll see far more by getting out of your car and going for a walk. Discovering birds in their natural habitats brings enjoyment and a deeper understanding of the birds themselves and the landscapes they inhabit.

Black-capped Chickadee
Poecile atricapillus

Like a sentinel, a black-capped chickadee sounds the predator alarm for others in the flock. The more *dee* notes in their *chickadee-dee-dee* cry, the higher the perceived peril. Researchers have discovered that pygmy owls provoke the most *dees,* up to 17.

Chickadees spend much of the day plucking small insects off of trees. When food is abundant, they hide seeds and can later remember thousands of their hiding places.

Black-capped chickadee, Alan Leftridge

Chickadees do not migrate but flock in foraging groups. Every autumn, some of their brain neurons containing old information die off and are replaced with new neurons that help them adapt to changes in their social flocks and their environment.

As you walk through the Black Hills' forests, listen for the high-pitch, two-tone call of the chickadee. Do they view you as a threat? Count the number of *dees* in their call.

Best Places to See Black-capped Chickadees
You will see chickadees throughout the Black Hills region. Look for them in Devils Tower National Monument, Mount Rushmore National Memorial, and around Deadwood.

Dark-eyed Junco
Junco hyemalis

Sometimes referred to as snowbirds, dark-eyed juncos are showy little sparrows that dart about the forest floors. You will certainly see juncos. They are the most abundant forest birds in the Black Hills. You

Dark-eyed junco, Alan Leftridge

can recognize them by their crisp markings and distinct white-lined tail feathers that fan out in flight. Juncos are primarily insectivores in summer, then switch to eating seeds in winter.

Best Places to See Dark-eyed Juncos

You can expect to see juncos in open places and forest margins throughout the Black Hills. They can be found from the prairie/forest margin up to the heights of Black Elk Peak. Look for them in Badlands National Park and Custer State Park.

Townsend's Solitaire
Myadestes townsendi

This flycatcher likes to nest on the ground. A year-round resident of the Black Hills, it sings throughout autumn and winter to establish and hold its summer territory. Although

Townsend's solitaire, Wind Cave NP, NPS photo

solitaires spend most days in the trees, you might see them darting into the open to catch insects. Winter finds them feasting almost exclusively on the berries of Rocky Mountain juniper trees. Survival rates favor those birds that fight for and defend the trees that have the most juniper berries.

Best Places to See Townsend's Solitaires
Look for Townsend's solitaires in Badlands National Park, around Pactola Reservoir, and in Spearfish Park and Spearfish Canyon.

Ruby-crowned Kinglet
Regulus calendula

Ruby-crowned kinglets seem hyperactive as they flutter among the foliage. About as long as the width of your hand, kinglets' elaborate and ringing songs refute their diminutive size and can be heard from afar. They flit about in treetops and in the brush, searching for spiders, aphids, wasps, ants, bark beetles, and other insects.

Best Places to See
Ruby-crowned Kinglets

Recognizable by their bright red crowns, you will find kinglets darting into view among the leaves of shrubby areas along roads and trails. Listen for loud bird calls in the bushes and fix your eyes on the location of the sound. A kinglet will eventually appear, showing its characteristic habit of nervous wing-flicking.

Ruby-crowned kinglet, NPS photo

Mountain bluebird, Neal Herbert, NPS photo

Mountain Bluebird
Sialia currucoides

Male mountain bluebirds are as vibrant as a Black Hills summer sky. But female mountain bluebirds are not impressed by the radiant azure males. They choose their mates, not by their superior looks or the excellence of their songs, but by the quality of the nesting site they offer. Both females and males prefer nesting in tree cavities, which are more common in old-growth trees. Few ideal places remain because of deforestation. Concerned people have placed nesting boxes in traditional bluebird habitat: the edges of meadows. The campaign is a success, with healthy stabilized populations throughout the Black Hills region.

Best Places to See Mountain Bluebirds

Look for mountain bluebirds in the open on perches such as treetops and fence posts, in the grasslands along the Wildlife Loop Road, Custer State Park, Devils Tower National Monument, Badlands National Park, and along the highways connecting the major features in the Black Hills region.

American Dipper
Cinclus mexicanus

Watch for bird droppings on the rocks in swift-running streams. This is a sign that dippers are in the area. You may hear their vocal *zeet,*

American dipper, Tim Rains, NPS photo

calling you to a gray bird with a short tail, the size of a young robin. Notice their bobbing action as they stand on the rocks above the water. They make their nests out of mosses near fast-moving water. Their sturdy yellow legs allow them to walk underwater to catch aquatic insects and larvae such as mayflies, caddis flies, and mosquitoes. Dippers are fun to watch as they walk into swiftly moving water and disappear. You can only guess where they will surface.

Best Places to See American Dippers

Dippers are year-round residents that live near fast-moving water in the warm months and move to lakes and larger rivers with open water during winter. Look for them along Spearfish Creek.

Western Tanager

Piranga ludoviciana

Western tanager, Jacob W. Frank, NPS photo

Male tanagers look like a flame in flight. Their near-parrot-like plumage gives western tanagers a striking contrast to their open evergreen forest habitat. During daylight, they search the upper reaches of the forest canopy branches for insects. An insect in the open is fair game as well. You can catch sight of one when it darts, flycatcher-style, to snatch an insect. Listen for a melodious robin-like song while walking in the Black Hills. Look up, and you might see a reclusive western tanager.

Best Places to See Western Tanagers

Watch for western tanagers in the lowland forests of Custer State Park, at Devils Tower National Monument, and in Badlands National Park.

Northern Flicker

Colaptes auratus

Northern flickers prefer to dig in the dirt and tear apart rotten logs to catch ants rather than climb trees like other woodpeckers. But, as other woodpeckers do, they excavate holes in dead or diseased tree trunks for nesting. Quaking aspens are a favored tree. They live in most types of forests, including those recently burned, riparian woods, and marsh edges. You may hear a northern flicker before seeing it. Like all woodpeckers, they drum on any object that produces the loudest noise.

Northern flicker, NPS photo

Best Places to See Northern Flickers

Look for northern flickers wherever you find old quaking aspen groves, especially in Badlands National Park.

Red-winged blackbird, Neal Herbert, NPS photo

Red-winged Blackbird
Agelaius phoeniceus

Their shoulders say so much. Male red-winged blackbirds use their striking red and yellow epaulets to display their intent. They attract females to their territory by hunching forward from a perched position, making their colors most brilliant. When resting, their wings are relaxed, displaying less of their epaulets, but just enough to ward off intruders. To get along with other blackbirds when communally feeding, they position their feathers so that no colors show. Flying back to their home in the cattail marshes, they once again display their bright colors.

Best Places to See Red-winged Blackbirds

Look for blackbirds along roadsides where water collects in ditches and marshes. In the springtime you will see red-winged blackbirds among the cattails. They are common in Badlands National Park, Custer State Park, and along roadways throughout the Black Hills region.

Western Meadowlark
Sturnella neglecta

From early spring through summer, you will hear the distinctive song of the western meadowlark. As its name implies, meadowlarks live in open meadows and the prairie regions of the Black Hills. Locating a male meadowlark is easy: look in the direction of its melodious voice. You will see a perched, robin-sized, yellow and black bird, singing on a fence post or tree snag. Its song—a rich, descending, warbling whistle—is territorial, and you can hear it over a half-mile away.

Best Places to See Western Meadowlarks

Listen for the western meadowlark as you drive through Badlands National Park, along

Western meadowlark,
Neal Herbert, NPS photo

Wildlife Loop Road in Custer State Park, and at Bear Butte and Devils Tower National Monument.

Gray jay, Neal Herbert, NPS photo

Gray Jay
Perisoreus canadensis

These medium-sized forest residents drift among the trees, and before you know it, a group has encircled your picnic table or campsite. Sometimes called "camp robbers," these sociable birds can become a problem as they try to take your food. They live in the Black Hills year-round. Nesting begins in March when snow may still be on the ground and temperatures fall as low as zero degrees F. Females protect the eggs with their thick down feathers and a well-insulated nest. They are omnivores that hoard food by using their sticky saliva to glue food bits to tree branches. You may be tempted to feed them, but it will cause an unrelenting commotion, and human food isn't good for them.

Best Places to See Gray Jays

Look for gray jays in the campgrounds and picnic areas in Custer State Park, Devils Tower National Monument, and around Sylvan Lake.

Steller's Jay
Cyanocitta stelleri

Like its eastern cousin, the blue jay, the Steller's jay is raucous. The bird's sounds are often mistaken for the screams of eagles and hawks. The jay's range of vocalizations is remarkably broad, including scratchy sounds, mimics of other birds, chirping

Steller's jay, Alan Leftridge

squirrels, meowing cats, wailing dogs, and even mechanical objects. Steller's jays are sociable, traveling in groups. Watch them playing or chasing each other within the forest canopy. They are year-round residents in the Black Hills, hiding pine seeds all summer for winter food. The seeds that they cannot locate often germinate, thereby revitalizing the forest.

Best Places to See Steller's Jays

Steller's jays live throughout the Black Hills forests and are often found where there is a closed forest canopy.

Black-billed magpie, Kristi DuBois, Montana Fish, Wildlife & Parks

Black-billed Magpie
Pica hudsonia

The Black Hills region is the eastern edge of this magpie's range. Coming from the east, many people are surprised the first time this colorful, long-tailed bird zips before their windshield. The bird may be racing to seize a small animal or insect. Magpies' menus are broad, including fruits, seeds, and even carrion. These showy kin of blue jays and crows create a steady stream of raucous cries when they gather over a meal.

Black-billed magpies are sociable, entertaining, and well adapted to people. Meriwether Lewis declared that magpies walked into their tents searching for food. Guard your food while picnicking or your meal will disappear in a feathered flash.

Best Places to See Black-billed Magpies

Magpies are omnivorous ground feeders that live in open woodlands and meadows. Look for them along the Wildlife Loop Road in Custer State Park, near roads and trails in Devils Tower National Monument, and as you travel I-90 and other roadways through the prairies.

Ruffed Grouse
Bonasa umbellus

You are on a day hike through a Black Hills forest that has dense underbrush. Without notice, a booming noise explodes from the leaves a few feet in front of you. Alarmed, you stop short. Is it a bear? No, more likely it was a ruffed grouse fleeing from you.

The grouse knew that you were approaching. But this bird, sometimes called a fool's hen, is well hidden on the forest floor, and it escapes danger only at the last moment. As you watch it escape, you notice it flies little better than a chicken. And if it lands on a tree limb, you will see it is not very good at standing in trees, either.

During the spring mating season, male grouse attract females with a low-pitched drumming of their wings while standing on a hollow log. It's

Ruffed grouse, Eric Johnston, NPS photo

fun to look for the male and watch as he performs the ritual. He begins by slowly beating his wings front to back as if intending to fly. In a few moments, the log echoes the sound of drumming that increases in speed.

Best Places to See Ruffed Grouse

Look and listen for a male grouse drumming as you hike the Black Elk Peak Trail.

Wild Turkey
Meleagris gallopavo

Turkeys are one of the most recognizable birds in the United States. They're popular around Thanksgiving, so we begin to learn about turkeys as children. Wild turkey populations diminished through the early 1900s, but

Wild turkeys, Alan Leftridge

transplant programs have spread wild turkeys to every state (even Hawaii) except Alaska. We also know that they have been around for a long time. Fossil turkey bones from Mexico and the southern United States have been dated to more than 5 million years old.

Best Places to See Wild Turkeys

Turkeys live in the open forests and at the margins of forests and meadows. Look for them as you travel Wildlife Loop Road in Custer State Park.

American Kestrel
Falco sparverius

Your eyes will never tire of seeing an American kestrel. This small falcon is found in more places than any other bird that inhabits the Black Hills. From Alaska to the tip of South America, kestrels live in open country, farmland,

American kestrel, NPS photo

forest edges, and even cities. Sometimes called "sparrow hawks," their diet includes small rodents and insects.

Look for kestrels perched atop posts and dead trees in the meadows and prairies of the Black Hills. You might see one hovering against a breeze before it dives to capture its prey.

Best Places to See American Kestrels

Kestrels are common in Badlands National Park, Custer State Park, Devils Tower National Monument, Bear Butte State Park, and Wind Cave National Park. They favor open grasslands and meadows with nearby perches in trees or on telephone lines.

Red-tailed hawk, Jim Peaco, NPS photo

Red-tailed Hawk
Buteo jamaicensis

You have heard the cry of red-tailed hawks many times. Hollywood movie directors have chosen the raucous cry of the red-tailed hawk to signify every kind of raptor, including bald eagles. It is the most common hawk species in the Black Hills, and possibly the most common hawk species in North America. They are found here year-round. These hawks vary in coloration, but most are a dark brown with a pale cream belly streaked with brown. In flight, the top of the tail is a distinctive rust or cinnamon color. Their wide-ranging diet includes voles, rabbits, snakes, frogs, other birds, and even insects.

Best Places to See Red-tailed Hawks

Red-tailed hawks patrol the grasslands, open woodlands, and agricultural fields. If you see a large bird slowly circling above, it may be a red-tailed hawk. Also, look for a chicken-size bird sitting on the fence posts and utility poles. It is likely a red-tailed hawk.

Osprey
Pandion haliaetus

One of nature's more thrilling shows is spotting an osprey in a vertical dive from great heights plunging into a lake and carrying a fish in its talons back to its nest. Once called fish hawks, they are

Osprey, Jim Peaco, NPS photo

unusual among birds because their menu is almost solely live fish.

Listen for the whistling or chirping calls of an osprey when you are near a lakeshore. The bird might be calling from its large nest atop a snag or while it is in flight. Look for its distinctive flight profile: a V-shaped wing silhouette. Watch one for a while, and wait to see if it locates a fish and dives for a meal.

Best Places to See Osprey

Osprey are common in the Black Hills area. You have a good chance of seeing them at Deerfield Lake, Sheridan Lake, and Pactola Reservoir.

Bald eagle, Alan Leftridge

Bald Eagle
Haliaeetus leucocephalus

The bald eagle's scientific name signifies a sea (*halo*) eagle (*aeetos*) with a white (*leukos*) head (*cephalus*). At the time of naming, "bald" meant "white," not hairless. The appointment of the bald eagle as the nation's symbol came in 1787. Proponents admired "its long life, great strength, and majestic looks." They were also believed to exist only on this continent. A spirited debate preceded the designation, as political leaders including Benjamin Franklin disapproved, stating that the eagle was of "bad moral character," proposing instead the turkey as the national bird.

Best Places to See Bald Eagles

Bald eagles primarily eat fish, so look for them around open water. You may also see eagles riding wind currents during their spring and fall migrations. In April through October you might see bald eagles along the George S. Mickelson Trail, at the Pactola Reservoir, and Deerfield Lake.

Golden Eagle
Aquila chrysaetos

What do Germany, Mexico, and Kazakhstan have in common? They each honor the golden eagle as their official national animal. In fact, the golden eagle is the most common national symbol in the world.

Golden eagles are impressive raptors. An adult has a wingspan greater than the width of your car! Their large wings allow them to dive from great heights, reaching close to 200 miles per hour as they stoop toward prey.

Golden eagles pursue meals of rabbits, ground squirrels, prairie dogs, and other small mammals, but they will also prey on larger animals like bighorn sheep lambs. After catching their meal, they often devour it at their nests. Their nests are made of branches and twigs and tend to be massive—about 6 feet wide and 3 feet deep. Golden eagles prefer to nest on cliffs, but they will also build in trees and on towers and nesting platforms.

Golden eagle, Neal Herbert, NPS photo

Best Places to See Golden Eagles

You may see golden eagles soaring above Badlands National Park, Wind Cave National Park, and Custer State Park.

A CHECKLIST OF BIRDS YOU MAY SEE OR HEAR	
_____ American Dipper	_____ Osprey
_____ American Kestral	_____ Red-tailed Hawk
_____ Bald Eagle	_____ Red-winged Blackbird
_____ Black-billed Magpie	_____ Ruby-crowned Kinglet
_____ Black-capped Chickadee	_____ Ruffed Grouse
_____ Dark-eyed Junco	_____ Steller's Jay
_____ Golden Eagle	_____ Townsend's Solitaire
_____ Gray Jay	_____ Western Meadowlark
_____ Mountain Bluebird	_____ Western Tanager
_____ Northern Flicker	_____ Wild Turkey

BEST WILDFLOWERS

The Black Hills region is a crossroads of mixed-grass prairie and Rocky Mountain ecosystems. Thanks to the region's diverse habitats and climates, hundreds of different blooming plants thrive here. Native plants, such as arrowleaf balsamroot, red columbine, and fireweed, are well adapted to growing conditions in the Black Hills. They are interwoven into their environment, drawing nutrients from the soil and providing good sources of nectar for native bees and other pollinators, and painting the hills with swaths of color.

Other plants are non-native imports brought here by humans, such as leafy spurge and musk thistle. Some have quickly expanded their range thanks to ideal growing conditions and few predators or diseases. These invasive foreign plants often outcompete native plant species for space and water. You can help prevent the spread of invasive plants by periodically checking your vehicles, clothing, packs, and shoes for any hitchhikers and disposing of them in trash receptacles.

Yarrow, Alan Leftridge

Yarrow
Achillea millefolium

Is it a weed or is it a flower? The answer depends on your association with yarrow. It seems to grow everywhere, taking over parcels of ground, even in manicured lawns. Yarrow is seen in meadows and along roadsides, as well as on dry, sunny slopes. It is an erect and fuzzy-stemmed perennial, with fern-like leaves, standing under three feet tall, and blooming between June and September.

The genus name, *Achillea*, is a reference to the ancient Greek hero, Achilles. Greek mythology suggests that he used a yarrow tincture either as protection from arrows or to heal wounds. Ironically, yarrow appears to actually slow blood clotting.

Best Places to See Yarrow
Yarrow can survive on dry or poor soils, but it is also found in moist areas. Look for it in meadows, gravelly areas, and along roadsides in Jewel Cave National Monument, Badlands National Park, Custer State Park, and Mount Rushmore National Memorial.

Oxalis
Oxalis spp.

The patch of Irish shamrock look-alikes you may have discovered are clusters of oxalis. It is also known as wood sorrel and false shamrock. There are more than 800 species that thrive worldwide. It is a rich source of vitamin C, and was a popular addition to sailors' diets to prevent scurvy. Today, its most common use is as a potted ornamental.

Best Places to See Oxalis
Oxalis grows well in the woodlands of Devils Tower National Monument and Custer State Park.

Oxalis, Alan Leftridge

Blue flax, Alan Leftridge

Blue Flax
Linum lewisii

Butterflies, bees, and flies love this perennial. First noted by the Corps of Discovery expedition in 1806, its species name honors one of the co-leaders, Meriwether Lewis. Blue flax grows throughout the West and has several local names, including wild blue flax, prairie flax, and Lewis flax. Blue flax prospers in poor, dry, sunny, often sandy soil. Although it grows up to two feet tall, look for it growing in small clumps leaning at an angle rather than upright. Blue flax blooms from May through September; each delicate blossom lasts only one day.

Best Places to See Blue Flax
You will find blue flax blooming all summer in woodland areas of Jewel Cave National Monument, Wind Cave National Park, and Devils Tower National Monument.

Harebell
Campanula rotundifolia

According to European folklore, harebells grew in places that hares

Harebell, Alan Leftridge

lived, and witches used the flower's juices to change themselves into hares. Scottish lore once referred to them as witches thimbles. A common North American name is bluebell.

Harebells grow in a variety of habitats. They enjoy full sun or shade, dry or moist soils. You will find them growing singly and in clumps with their flowers hanging on thin stalks up to a foot tall.

Best Places to See Harebells

You will discover harebells in forests and meadows, among cliffs, in roadside gravel, and along lake beaches. Look for them around the shores of Sylvan Lake and Legion Lake in Custer State Park. Harebells are also common in the riparian areas of Jewel Cave National Monument, Devils Tower National Monument, and Wind Cave National Park.

Sticky Geranium
Geranium viscosissimum

Sticky geranium, Alan Leftridge

Sticky hairs cover the stems and lower leaves of this geranium. Avoid handling the plant or you will need to scrub the gumminess off your hands. The gluey substance has enzymes found in carnivorous plants, leading some botanists to think that the sticky geranium is evolving in that direction. After flowering, its seeds develop in an elongated capsule that looks like a crane's bill. When the capsule dries, it splits, flinging seeds away at high speed, spreading the range of the plants.

Best Places to See Sticky Geraniums

Expect to find sticky geraniums flowering May to September throughout open woods and meadows. They can be plentiful along creek banks, grassy openings, and roadsides.

Wild Rose
Rosa acicularis

This native wild rose has attractive pink blooms, thorns, and, in winter, large red fruit called hips. Some people make jelly or wine from the outer husk of the rose hips, which are rich in vitamins A and C. Several species of wildlife benefit from the nutritional

Wild rose, Badlands NP, NPS photo

properties of the wild rose. Mule deer and white-tailed deer, pronghorn, elk, and mountain sheep browse the leaves and twigs. Black bears, rabbits, small mammals, and numerous songbirds consume rose hips.

Best Places to See Wild Roses
Wild rose plants mingle among Black Hills spruce, paper birch, and quaking aspen trees. Look for roses blossoming in open forests, on riverbanks, and in clearings throughout the Black Hills region, especially in Badlands National Park in spring. You will also find a wild rose emblem adorning license plates on vehicles from Alberta, Canada.

Fireweed, Alan Leftridge

Fireweed
Chamerion angustifolium

This plant has several names, including fireweed, great willowherb, and rosebay willowherb. It was known as bombweed in England after World War II because it quickly sprouted in bomb craters. Fireweed gets its North American name for growing in burnt sites. The plant's rapid colonization brings striking pink color to burnt areas and roadsides, rejuvenating disturbed soils and increasing nutrients essential for plant succession. Autumn is a good time to witness fireweed seeds as they float considerable distances across the Black Hills landscape. Once established, fireweed provides food for deer and elk.

Best Places to See Fireweed
Look for fireweed blooming along the roads and trails throughout the Black Hills from late June through September.

Calypso orchid, Jacob W. Frank, NPS photo

Calypso Orchid

Calypso bulbosa

This small, lovely, and pink orchid is also known as fairy slipper, or lady's slipper. The names suggest delicate beauty. In Greek mythology, Calypso was also beautiful. The daughter of Atlas, she lived on the island of Ogygia, where she beguiled Odysseus to remain with her for several years. These orchids live no more than five years and are becoming as rare as their preferred habitat—mature forests. They are susceptible to disturbances. So if you find a patch, tread lightly. As with all wildflowers, please don't pick them.

Best Places to See Calypso Orchids

Calypso orchids are difficult to spot among the other plant life of the forest floor. Look for them blooming during May and June in cool, deep-shaded forests.

Seep Monkeyflower

Mimulus guttatus

This flower's common name refers to the

Seep monkeyflower, Chelsea Monks, Black Hills National Forest blossom's resemblance to a monkey's face. The genus name, *Mimulus,* implies an actor in a farce or mime, and the species name, *guttatus,* means "spotted," referring to the bloom's orange spots. Monkeyflowers' favored habitats are near creeks, along stream banks, and in riparian meadows.

Best Places to See Seep Monkeyflowers

You will find these bright flowers blooming from May to September in the riparian habitats of Wind Cave National Park.

Black-eyed Susan, Alan Leftridge

Black-eyed Susan
Rudbeckia hirta

Black-eyed Susans are pioneer plants. Their seeds are among the first to germinate after a fire. Then, they live for only two years. Whether in full sun or partial shade, they bloom profusely during their short life, adding cheerful splashes of gold to the landscape. Rabbits and deer eat this prolific wildflower. Butterflies and bees are attracted to blanketed fields of black-eyed Susans.

Best Places to See Black-eyed Susans

Black-eyed Susans bloom June to October in the prairies, along roadsides, and in disturbed areas in the Black Hills. You will recognize them by their chocolate brown to dark purple center. Look for them in Wind Cave National Park and Jewel Cave National Monument growing in riparian and woodland environments.

Arrowleaf Balsamroot
Balsamorhiza sagittata

The blooms of this long-lived perennial give one of the first signs that spring has arrived in the Black Hills. It is easily recognized from a distance by its large, showy, yellow flowers spangling hillsides in early May. First collected by Meriwether Lewis in 1806, its big green leaves resemble the shape of arrowheads. The

Arrowleaf balsamroot, Alan Leftridge

complete plant is edible, from flower-top to deep taproot. The seeds are eaten by birds and rodents. Mule deer, white-tailed deer, elk, pronghorn, and bighorn sheep readily consume the stems, leaves, and flowers.

Best Places to See Arrowleaf Balsamroot

Look for the bright yellow flowers on open hillsides, prairies, and mountain meadows throughout the Black Hills region, especially in the open areas of Devils Tower National Monument and Bear Butte State Park.

Prairie Coneflower

Ratibida columnifera

This striking plant is also known as red coneflower and Mexican hat. The flowers sit atop leafless stems that can reach three feet tall. Prairie coneflowers are a favorite of a wide variety of bees as well as flies, wasps, butterflies, and beetles. The seed heads provide food for birds in late fall. Like all native prairie flora, prairie coneflowers are fire dependent. Periodic burns from lightning strikes kill invasive competitors and add nutrients to soils, which favors native flora like the prairie coneflower.

Prairie coneflower,
Wind Cave NP, NPS photo

Best Places to See Prairie Coneflowers

During summer, you will find the colorful prairie coneflowers growing in Black Hills' woodlands, along roadsides, and on the prairie east to Badlands National Park.

Yellow Coneflower

Ratibida pinnata

Once established, these perennials can grow up to four feet tall, tickling the bellies of Black Hills bison.

Like prairie coneflowers, yellow coneflowers benefit from periodic burning from lightning-sparked fires. In case cyclic fires do not occur, coneflowers secrete chemicals through their roots that suppress the growth of neighboring grasses.

Yellow coneflower, Alan Leftridge

Best Places to See Yellow Coneflowers

Look for yellow coneflowers in the prairies around the Black Hills, on the margins of forests, along roadsides, and in Badlands National Park and Devils Tower National Monument in late summer.

Blanket flower, Wind Cave NP, NPS photo

Blanket Flower
Gaillardia aristata

The blanket flower is a member of the sunflower family, and native to the Black Hills region. Its banded combinations of vibrant yellow, red, and orange might attract you from afar. As you can imagine, it is a favorite of nectar-seeking butterflies. There are two traditional accounts for the common name. One explanation is that the flowers resemble the patterns of Native American blankets, the other is that some botanists describe the plants as growing colonies that blanket the ground.

Best Places to See Blanket Flowers

Look for blooming blanket flowers throughout the Black Hills region in open meadows, prairies, on foothills, and along roadsides. Depending on the elevation, they bloom from spring to autumn.

Red Columbine
Aquilegia canadensis

This perennial has plenty of cousins. There are between 60 and 70 species of columbine growing in North America. The common name columbine comes from the Latin for "dove," because of the resemblance to five doves clustered together in the inverted flower. The

Red columbine, Alan Leftridge

flowers attract hummingbirds and insects that hover. It also attracted Thomas Jefferson, who is said to have cultivated it at Monticello.

Best Places to See Red Columbine

Look for red columbine flowers in open and shaded woods, usually near water, in Custer State Park.

Paintbrush

Castilleja spp.

Paintbrush grows in many colors, including red, orange, yellow, and white. This favorite perennial is named for its colorful, ragged bracts that appear to have been dipped in paint. Observe the flower design and you will see there is no place for pollinators to land. Paintbrush requires hovering insects and birds for pollination. Hummingbirds seek its nectar, leading some botanists to theorize that paintbrush plants and hummingbirds co-evolved.

Paintbrush, Alan Leftridge

Best Places to See Paintbrush

The open woods, meadows, and roadsides of the Black Hills are ablaze with paintbrush from April to September.

BEST TREES

Think of the Black Hills area as a sea of grass lapping against a forested island. The most familiar evergreen tree species on this isle is the ponderosa pine. The darkness of these trees seen from a distance led to the Lakota name, *Paha Sapa*—Black Hills. In higher elevations you will find thick stands of Black Hills spruce trees. Moist areas of the region sustain a mixture of deciduous trees. Quaking aspen, bur oak, paper birch, and plains cottonwood trees are abundant in some drainages and along permanent stream banks. In total, twelve major tree species populate the Black Hills.

Black Hills spruce, Alan Leftridge

Black Hills Spruce
Picea glauca var. *densata*

You may be familiar with the unpleasant prickliness of spruce tree needles, but the Black Hills spruce's needles are soft to the touch. The chewable foliage is eaten by rabbits and deer, red squirrels devour the cones and new shoots, and black bears and porcupines feast on the bark.

The Black Hills spruce is a close cousin of the white spruce. It evolved in the Black Hills area of South Dakota and northeast Wyoming.

The slow-growing trees can live 350 years, reaching up to 50 feet tall and 25 feet wide. Its lovely conical form and dark green needles inspired South Dakota lawmakers to select it as the state tree.

Best Places to Find Black Hills Spruce
In the wild, Black Hills spruce grow on sunny slopes above 5,000 feet. You will find several specimens in Spearfish Canyon growing around the Latchstring Inn and Spearfish Canyon Lodge.

Ponderosa Pine
Pinus ponderosa

Ponderosa pines evolved to take advantage of periodic fires that keep other trees from

Ponderosa pine, USDA Forest Service

growing in their forest. They annually shed masses of their long needles that, once dried, burn with ease. Frequent ground fires kill trees that compete with ponderosas for water and nutrients. With few lower branches for ground fires to reach and a thick bark that insulates the trunks from heat, a stand of ponderosa trees can survive into a mature forest.

Mature ponderosas are sometimes called yellow pines because of the color of their trunk.

They can grow to 225 feet tall and 25 feet in diameter, and live up to 500 years.

Look for a tree with jigsaw puzzle-like bark. Take a whiff of the tree trunk. Can you detect a fragrance? If you note a soft vanilla or a butter-scotch scent, you have identified a ponderosa pine.

Best Places to Find Ponderosa Pines

Ponderosa pines blanket the Black Hills. They are the trees that give the area its distinctive dark appearance and inspired the Lakota people to call the mountains *Paha Sapa,* meaning the "hills that are black."

Rocky Mountain Juniper
Juniperus scopulorum

Food and shelter, what else can you ask for in a tree? In the Black Hills' wide-open places, Rocky Mountain junipers provide needed food and shelter for animals and birds.

Pronghorn, bighorn sheep, mule deer, and white-tailed deer browse on juniper foliage and twigs. Cedar waxwings and small mammals eat the bluish-black, berry-like fruit in autumn and winter.

The junipers furnish critical nesting and

Rocky Mountain juniper, Alan Leftridge

year-round shelter. Several kinds of birds use the trees for roosting protection and nesting. The trees are valuable cover in the winter for pronghorn, elk, mule deer, white-tailed deer, small mammals, and myriad birds. Because of the dense growing pattern of the branches, they provide shelter from snowstorms.

Rocky Mountain juniper trees range in size from a shrub to 30-foot trees. They enjoy dry habitats. Stands of Rocky Mountain juniper grow well on ridges, cliffs, and dry, rocky hillsides.

Best Places to Find Rocky Mountain Junipers

Look for Rocky Mountain junipers growing singly and in small groves in the dry areas of Custer State Park, Bear Butte, and Badlands National Park.

Bur oak, Wind Cave NP, NPS photo

Bur Oak
Quercus macrocarpa

The bur oak's acorns are up to 1.5 inches long, making them the largest of any acorns native to North America. Do not expect to find many acorns under the trees, unless you have discovered the massive nut crop that occurs only every few years. That is when the trees exhibit an evolutionary process known as masting. They drop an excessive amount of acorns, and seed eaters cannot consume them all. The profusion of acorns ensures the survival of some seeds, and the next generation of bur oaks.

Bur oaks are vital to wildlife needs in the Black Hills region. They provide crucial habitat for birds and some mammals, and a smorgasbord of nourishment for many animals. Porcupines and deer eat the leaves, bark, and twigs, and acorns provide food for squirrels, deer, and large birds.

Best Places to Find Bur Oak

Look for bur oaks growing in open areas, often near waterways. There are several specimens by the State Game Lodge in Custer State Park.

Plains Cottonwood
Populus deltoides ssp. monilifera

The plains cottonwood is the Wyoming state tree. A member of the willow family that includes aspens and poplars, the plains cottonwood produces a cotton-like mass surrounding its seeds, making it easy for them to float away in a soft Black Hills' breeze.

Plains cottonwood, Wind Cave NP, NPS photo

The seeds that make their way to moist, well-drained soils can germinate. Once established, they are fast growing, reaching up to 60 to 80 feet tall and 50 feet in diameter. Each autumn finds mature trees with golden yellow leaves that shimmer in the sunshine like aspen leaves.

Best Places to Find Plains Cottonwood

Plains cottonwood grow throughout the Black Hills region along most of the rivers and streams and in open meadows. Look for them in Custer State Park, along the Belle Fourche River in Devils Tower National Monument, and near the Wind Cave Visitor Center.

Quaking Aspen
Populus tremuloides

Quaking aspen, William Dunmire, NPS photo

Look for low-lying, dome-shaped groves of deciduous trees throughout the Black Hills. These groves are of quaking aspen, the most widely distributed tree species in North America. Their seeds can float great distances on the wind. Once the seeds germinate in moist areas, the saplings begin to colonize. Thereafter, they propagate by sending their roots outward from the older trees in the center. The leaves of these genetically identical tree islands shimmer with bursts of yellow and orange each autumn, setting the Black Hills ablaze in swaths of colored grandeur.

Best Places to Find Quaking Aspen

Aspen grow wherever there is running water. You will find small groves along Wildlife Loop Road in Custer State Park.

A CHECKLIST OF THE BEST TREES	
_____ Black Hills Spruce	_____ Ponderosa Pine
_____ Bur Oak	_____ Quaking Aspen
_____ Plains Cottonwood	_____ Rocky Mountain Juniper

BEST ACTIVITIES FOR CHILDREN

Play time at Sheridan Lake,
Gary Chancey, Black Hills National Forest

Writing in *The Sense of Wonder*, Rachel Carson observed, "If a child is to keep alive his inborn sense of wonder . . . he needs the companionship of at least one adult who can share it, discovering with him the joy, excitement, and mystery of the world we live in."

The Black Hills offer more than exceptional scenery. It is like no other place in America for family fun. The region's rich natural and cultural heritage can inspire young and old alike to engage with nature, other cultures, and history. Here is a list of places you can take your children to spark their curiosity, reveal wonders, and build lasting memories.

- Mount Rushmore National Memorial: Celebrate American patriotism.
- Crazy Horse Memorial: Honor Native American heritage.
- Reptile Gardens: Discover unique reptiles and exotic plants.
- Buffalo Gap National Grassland: Experience the great American prairie.
- Journey Museum: Learn about the Black Hills' natural and cultural histories.
- Minuteman Missile National Historic Site: The Cold War on display.
- South Dakota Air and Space Museum: Big, historic airplanes that your kids will love.

Learning about watersheds,
Bethany Doten, Black Hills National Forest

- Black Hills Central Railroad: A two-hour ride that your child will always remember!
- Dinosaur Park: Seven dinosaurs overlook Rapid City. Kids love this place.

- Broken Boot Gold Mine tour: Search for gold like a miner.

- Badlands National Park: Enjoy grand vistas and outstanding geological features.

- Black Hills Playhouse: World-class theater entertainment.

Dinosaur Park, Chad Coppess, South Dakota Tourism

Go on a Photo Safari

Put that Smartphone or digital camera to a good educational use. Help your kids organize their photos into a story about their vacation or a particular outing. Select a theme like "Patterns of Custer State Park." Help your child to see and capture images of patterns, such as patterns in plant growth, types of flowers, tree leaves, where animals are found, lichen growth, clouds, weather, and where people go and gather. Encourage them to post their story on their favorite social media site. Want a topic other than patterns? Possibilities abound—change, adaptation, interdependence, similarities, differences, or create your own theme.

Attend an Evening Program

Kids love attending evening programs. Help them learn about the fascinating cultural and natural history diversity of the Black Hills with a park ranger. Programs are offered in Mount Rushmore National Memorial, Wind Cave National Park, Jewel Cave National Monument, Badlands National Park, Devils Tower National Monument, and Custer State Park.

Topics include bears, birds, history, climate change, the night sky, geology, and more. Presentations are at campground amphitheaters, visitor centers, and in caves. Check the park newspapers for specific topics, times, and locations.

Join in a Ranger-led Hike

Many ranger-led programs are uniquely designed for youth and families. Inquire at the visitor centers of Devils Tower National Monument, Badlands National Park, Wind Cave National Park, Jewel Cave National Monument, and Mount Rushmore National Memorial for a schedule of ranger-led interpretive hikes.

Become a Junior Ranger

Explore, learn, and protect as a Junior Ranger! Children attend a ranger-led program and complete at least five activities in a Junior Ranger booklet. The booklets are available at visitor centers in the parks. Park units participating in the program include:

- Badlands National Park: get your Junior Ranger booklet at the Ben Reifel Visitor Center.
- Wind Cave National Park: booklets are available in the visitor center bookstore.
- Jewel Cave National Monument: two programs, inquire at the visitor center.
- Mount Rushmore National Memorial: booklets are available at the visitor center and the bookstore.
- Devils Tower National Monument: booklets are at the visitor center.

Discovering fossils, Badlands NP, NPS photo

Junior Ranger badges and certificates are awarded when a park ranger reviews the booklet and has a brief interview with your child. Junior Ranger materials are available for ages 5 and up.

Your child can also participate online at the National Park Service's WebRangers site: www.nps.gov/webrangers/.

Take a Walk

Do you want to explore the Black Hills with your child without a guide? The Black Hills has hundreds of miles of trails. Start with short, educational, and exciting walks that will inspire your child to learn. Consider self-guided trails that have interpretive brochures at the trailheads. Make sure that you bring snacks and water.

Devils Tower National Monument

- Tower Trail, paved 1.3-mile loop.

The trail takes you through a ponderosa pine forest and a boulder field. Tired feet can find relief at benches along the trail. Signs interpret the area's geology and ecology. Please do not touch cloth swatches or small bundles tied to the trees. They are Native American prayer cloths and represent the spiritual connection many people have with the tower.

Mount Rushmore National Memorial

🐾 Presidential Trail, 1.3-mile loop.

Get up close to feel the grandeur of the colossal sculpture. Be aware that the walk requires navigating 422 steps; make sure that you and your child are capable and up for the challenge. The reward is a lifetime memory.

Black Hills National Forest

🐾 Roughlock Trail, 2 miles round trip.

This paved trail in Spearfish Canyon takes you to spectacular Roughlock Falls. Children delight in looking for wildflowers and wildlife in the canyon. Bring a picnic for your destination and watch for American dippers along the banks of the cold, rushing waters below the waterfall. The trailhead is behind Spearfish Canyon Lodge in Savoy.

🐾 Devil's Bathtub Trail, 1.3-mile loop.

The trailhead is south of Spearfish, at the start of Spearfish Canyon Scenic Byway.

Roughlock Falls, Chelsea Monks, Black Hills National Forest

The trail enters a narrow limestone corridor and follows the creek to the Devil's Bathtub. Make sure that your child is willing and able to get wet, because the trail crosses the creek several times. Pack a picnic and let your child play among the rocks and take a dip in the Devil's Bathtub pool.

🐾 Little Spearfish Falls, 1.5 miles round trip.

This trail is an excellent choice for a short walk through a ponderosa/Black Hills spruce forest. Your destination is 70-foot Little Spearfish Falls in Spearfish Canyon. The trailhead is behind the Latchstring Inn Restaurant in Savoy.

Custer State Park

🐾 Sylvan Lake Shore Trail, 1-mile loop.

Sylvan Lake Shore Trail is one of the easiest and prettiest hikes in Custer State Park. This trail makes a loop around the lake, affording walkers wonderful views of the gigantic granite rocks in and around the lake. This extremely easy walk is fun for everyone.

Wind Cave National Park

🐾 Elk Mountain Nature Trail, 1.2-mile loop.

Pick up a pamphlet guide at the trailhead and read aloud as you visit the nine stops along this short trail. You will share with your child the diversity of life in three different ecosystems, and how fire plays an important role in nature.

Jewel Cave National Monument

🐾 A Walk on the Roof Trail, 0.25-mile loop.

Waiting for your scheduled tour? This 30-minute walk is a great way to encourage your children to imagine what is below their feet. They will soon find out. The trail wanders through ponderosa pine forest with a view of the nearby canyons.

Badlands National Park

🐾 Door Trail, 0.75 mile round trip.

This is the first trail you encounter if entering the park from SD 240 south of Exit 131 on I-90. Give your child an introduction to the Badlands by taking them on this easy walk to a place called the Door. It will give them a first view of the outstanding landscape.

Fort Meade Recreation Area

🐾 The Alkali Creek Nature Trail, 1 mile round trip.

This is a perfect trail for small children. The walk is through prairie, forest, and back to Alkali Creek. Pick up a pamphlet at the trailhead and read aloud the interpretive messages at each of the stops.

Read Aloud

Be prepared. A rainy day or a lull in activities gives you an opportunity to read a book with your child. Many entertaining and informative books are available at the various park visitor centers. Pick some that you want to read and that will give your child a better understanding of the Black Hills' natural and cultural heritage.

Here are some of the many available books that will enhance a child's experiences:

🐾 *Black Bear Babies!,* Donald M. Jones (ages 0-3)
🐾 *Dakota Babies!* (ages 0-3)

> *Be a Park Ranger,* Robert Rath (ages 2 and up)
> *How Do Bears Sleep?,* E. J. Bird (ages 2 and up)
> *The Cutest Critter,* Marion Bauer and Stan Tekiela (ages 2 and up)
> *Lost in the Woods,* Carl R. Sams II and Jean Stoick (ages 2 and up)
> *Lil' MacDonald Likes to Hike,* Jennifer Taylor Tormalehto (ages 4 and up)
> *Four Famous Faces,* Jean L. S. Patrick (ages 4 and up)
> *Who Carved the Mountain?,* Jean L. S. Patrick (ages 7 and up)
> *Who Pooped in the Black Hills?,* Gary Robson (ages 5-8)
> *Tales of the Black Hills,* Helen Rezatto (ages 5 and up)
> *A Child's Introduction to the Night Sky,* Michael Driscoll and Meredith Hamilton (ages 8 and up)
> *National Geographic Kids National Parks Guide U.S.A.* (ages 8 and up)

Most of these books are available through the Mount Rushmore Society, www.mountrushmore.com, (607) 574-1333.

Ride a Horse

Give your children a sense of what it must have been like to see the Black Hills before people used automobiles as their primary source of transportation. Rides are 1 and 2 hours through the beautiful Black Hills countryside. Private outfitters offer rides for those 8 years old and up. Blue Bell Stables, Hollingsworth Horses, and Rockin' R Rides are near Custer. Triple R Ranch is close to Keystone, The Stables is outside Hill City, and Andy's Trail Rides is located at Lead. Call ahead for reservations and to get specifics on ages, times, distances, and costs.

Reflect

Today's fast-paced, gadget-filled lifestyle is busy with distractions. The Black Hills presents wonderful opportunities to take a deep breath and reconnect with the natural world. Find a quiet, peaceful spot. Challenge your child to sit in solitude for 5 or 10 minutes (try it yourself!). Ask them to think about what they hear, smell, and see. Encourage them to write or draw a picture about the experience and what their senses revealed to them. As they settle in for the night, ask your child to reflect on what they liked about the day's activities.

View the Night Sky

More than 80 percent of Americans live in cities and suburbs. Living in the glow of urban lights, children do not experience the excitement of seeing the Milky Way, August's Perseids meteor shower, or summer constellations. Devils Tower National Monument, Badlands National Park, Custer State Park, Wind Cave National Park, and Jewel Cave National Monument have dark nighttime skies that are excellent for stargazing. Do it on your own, or attend one of the Night Sky programs offered throughout the summer by park rangers in Badlands National Park. The night sky inspires awe in a child, and its mysteries are brought to light when a family member takes the time to share in the discovery.

Night sky, Neal Herbert, NPS photo

BEST THINGS TO DO ON A RAINY (OR SNOWY) DAY

You plan your vacation hoping for the best weather. But sometimes nature doesn't cooperate. What to do on days with unexpected weather? Here are a few places to visit.

Journey Museum

This downtown Rapid City jewel is housed in a gorgeous building and packed with exhibits and displays presenting the geography and human events that have shaped the Black Hills region. The museum is open daily, year-round.

Stormy weather, Shaina Niehans, NPS photo

The Journey Museum & Learning Center
222 New York Street
Rapid City, SD 57701
(605) 394-6923
www.journeymuseum.org

Journey Museum, Alan Leftridge

The Mammoth Site

The Mammoth Site is an interactive experience for young and old. Take a tour to learn about how dozens of mammoths got trapped in a sinkhole thousands of years ago. Explore the exhibit hall surrounding the indoor dig site. See paleontologists excavating the hapless creatures' remains. Surprise your kids with a one or two-hour excavation with a paleontologist. Open daily during the summer.

The Mammoth Site
1800 US Hwy 18 Bypass
Hot Springs, SD 57747
(605) 745-6017
www.mammothsite.com

Evans Plunge

Get wet! The water in the plunge is guaranteed to be warmer than the rain outside. The 87-degree F. mineral water has attracted bathers for generations, making Evans Plunge the oldest tourist attraction in the Black Hills. There is plenty of room for swimming in the 50-by-200-foot spring-fed pool. Kids enjoy the slides and Tarzan rings.

Evans Plunge
1145 N. River Street
Hot Springs, SD 57747
(605) 745-5165
www.evansplunge.com

Black Hills Mining Museum

Learn how to pan for gold with guaranteed good luck. Interpretive staff members will lead you on a tour of a simulated underground mine. Mining history in the Black Hills comes alive through the museum's exhibits. Gold lured throngs of people to the Black Hills. Learn about its allure and how people have extracted it from the earth.

Black Hills Mining Museum
323 W. Main Street
Lead, SD 57785
(605) 584-1605
bhminingmuseum@rushmore.com

Homestake Mine, Alan Leftridge

Sanford Lab Homestake Visitor Center

The histories of the Homestake Mine and the town of Lead come alive in the visitor center's exhibits. Learn how the 370 miles of mine tunnels are used today to study the subatomic wonders of the universe. Open daily for you to explore.

> Sanford Lab Homestake Visitor Center
> 160 W. Main Street
> Lead, SD 57754
> (605) 584-3110
> www.sanfordlabhomestake.com

South Dakota Air and Space Museum

Spend a morning roaming the galleries and exhibits about America's aviation history. The museum showcases over thirty military aircraft from World War II to modern day. You can take a 50-minute bus tour of Ellsworth Air Force Base and the Delta 9 Minuteman missile silo to learn more about the Cold War.

> South Dakota Air and Space Museum
> 2890 Rushmore Drive
> Ellsworth Air Force Base, SD 57706
> (605) 385-5189
> www.sdairandspacemuseum.com

Adams Museum, Alan Leftridge

Adams Museum

The Black Hills' oldest museum, the Adams, showcases artifacts and displays of Deadwood's legendary past. It is a "must-visit" during a tour of the city. Learn about the colorful lives of Wild Bill, Calamity Jane, Potato Creek Johnny, Seth Bullock, and imaginary figures like Deadwood Dick. The museum is open year-round.

> Adams Museum
> 54 Sherman Street
> Deadwood, SD 57732
> (605) 578-1714
> www.deadwoodhistory.com

Sturgis Motorcycle Museum

This museum honors the history of motorcycling with exhibits that showcase motorcycle models through the years. Galleries include Early Days, British, Modern, and Bikes on Loan. The museum pays tribute to the annual Sturgis Motorcycle Rally. Open year-round.

> Sturgis Motorcycle Museum
> 999 Main Street
> Sturgis, SD 57785
> (605) 347-2001
> www.sturgismuseum.com

Historic Elks Theatre

A great way to pass a rainy afternoon is to catch a matinee at the Historic Elks Theatre in downtown Rapid City. Check what's playing at www.elkstheatre.com.

> Elks Theatre
> 512 6th Street
> Rapid City, SD 57701
> (605) 343-7888
> www.elkstheatre.com

WINTER IN THE BLACK HILLS

Visualize an enchanted scene in which the trees and mountains before you are blanketed in sparkling snow. The morning after a passing storm is often cloudless, calm, and cold, offering a sublime spectacle. Few visitors experience the Black Hills at these times, but you can plan to create your own memories of winter that a camera can only partially capture.

Snowshoeing, Beth Steinhauer, Black Hills National Forest

January and February are the coldest winter months here. Daytime highs range in the 30s F., while lows average between 10 to 20 degrees F. Below-zero readings are common in the higher valleys of the Black Hills.

Snowfall varies throughout the Black Hills region. Snow on the plains usually melts in a few days. The average annual snowfall in places like Hot Springs is 27 inches, while Lead approaches 200 inches. The deeper snow totals provide excellent winter recreation conditions.

Depending on the elevation, winter hiking conditions are best through December. After then, enough snow usually accumulates for traditional winter sports: cross-country skiing, alpine skiing and snowboarding, snowshoeing, and snowmobiling. Deep freezes allow for ice skating and ice fishing.

Snowmobiling, Beth Steinhauer, Black Hills National Forest

Do you cross-country ski or snowshoe? If so, the Black Hills region is for you. Many backcountry roads become impassable to vehicles due to snow. January, February, and March are excellent cross-country skiing and snowshoeing months. Long-distance enthusiasts seek the 109-mile George S.

Mickelson Trail for its relatively flat terrain.

Alpine ski enthusiasts head for Terry Peak Ski Area and Deer Mountain Ski Resort to carve and shred their way down the slopes.

Fishing doesn't end with the warmer weather. Anglers head for their favorite spots once ice thickens enough to

Cross-country skiing, Beth Steinhauer, Black Hills National Forest

support their weight. Popular ice fishing areas are Deerfield Lake, Pactola Lake, and Sheridan Lake. Don't like the winter weather? Go underground. Wind Cave National Park and Jewel Cave National Monument offer tours all winter. The average temperature in Wind Cave is 55 degrees F, while Jewel Cave maintains 49 degrees F.

Ice fishing, Gary Chancey, Black Hills National Forest

Ice skating is allowed on all lakes in the Black Hills National Forest. None of the lakes are groomed.

The Black Hills' many museums are great destinations on a winter's day. The Adams Museum in Deadwood, Journey Museum in Rapid City, and Sanford Lab in Lead are excellent choices for enriching your knowledge about the natural and cultural heritages of the Black Hills.

The Black Hills are always accessible. There are many tourist opportunities for you to choose, whatever the season!

BEST PLACES TO LISTEN TO MUSIC

Add to your experience by sampling regional music. Throughout the summer you will find taverns and other venues offering music. There are two places that consistently provide entertainment: Main Street Square in the Rapid City Historic Business District and the Crazy Horse Memorial.

Rapid City Historic Business District

The district is lively, featuring weekly summer music festivals, scheduled live concerts, and street musicians. Visit www.downtownrapidcity.com and www.mainstreetsquare.com for current information.

Crazy Horse Memorial

The Crazy Horse Memorial Welcome Center offers ongoing Native American music and dance demonstrations at the outdoor pavilion or indoors. Inquire about programs and times at (605) 673-4681, memorial@crazyhorse.org.

Native dance, Crazy Horse Memorial, Alan Leftridge

BEST BOOKS ABOUT THE BLACK HILLS

Many of these publications are available through the Mount Rushmore Society, www.mountrushmore.com, (607) 574-1333.

Good Reads

- *The Spring Creek Chronicles*, Dick Kettlewell
- *Deadwood Saints and Sinners,* Jerry L. Bryant and Barbara Fifer
- *Bad Boys of the Black Hills...And Some Wild Women, Too,* Barbara Fifer
- *The Lakota and the Black Hills: The Struggle for Sacred Ground,* Jeffrey Ostler
- *Bury My Heart at Wounded Knee: An Indian History of the American West,* Dee Brown
- *Black Elk Speaks,* John G. Neihardt
- *Exploring with Custer: The 1874 Black Hills Expedition,* Ernest Grafe and Paul Horsted
- *Crazy Horse: The Lakota Warrior's Life and Legacy,* the Edward Clown Family as told to William B. Matson
- *Wild Bill Hickok & Calamity Jane: Deadwood Legends,* James D. McLaird
- *One Man's Dream: The History of the Black Hills Playhouse, Custer State Park, Black Hills of South Dakota, 1946-1995,* Dorothy Ross Delicate

- *The Civilian Conservation Corps in and Around the Black Hills,* Peggy Sanders
- *Ghost Towns and Other Historical Sites of the Black Hills,* Bruce A. Raisch
- *Seth Bullock: Black Hills Lawman,* David A. Wolff

Photography

- *Black Hills Impressions,* Dick Kettlewell
- *South Dakota Wildlife Impressions,* Dick Kettlewell
- *South Dakota Simply Beautiful,* J. C. Leacock
- *Black Hills Vintage Postcard Book,* Farcountry Press

Fun for Kids

- *Who Pooped in the Black Hills,* Gary Robson and Robert Rath
- *Bison,* Cherie Winner
- *Dakota Babies!*

ICONIC SUBJECTS TO PHOTOGRAPH

Badlands NP, Alan Leftridge

If this is your first trip to the Black Hills, you likely will be taking pictures of everything that attracts your interest. Here are some of the most iconic images you may want to capture and share with your family and friends back home.

____ Mount Rushmore National Memorial
____ Crazy Horse Memorial
____ Devils Tower
____ Badlands landscapes
____ Bear Butte
____ Sylvan Lake
____ Legion Lake
____ Needles landscapes
____ Needles Eye
____ Pigtail bridges, Iron Mountain Road
____ Deadwood architecture
____ Main Street Square, Rapid City
____ Bullock Hotel
____ Mount Moriah Cemetery (especially the graves
of Wild Bill and Calamity Jane)
____ Wildlife Loop Road

_____ Bison
_____ Pronghorn
_____ Prairie dogs
_____ Spearfish Canyon
_____ Bridal Veil Falls
_____ Roughlock Falls

The best times to photograph these features are before 10 A.M. and after 4 P.M. in order to avoid deep, contrasting shadows. Many professional photographers look for clear skies the morning following a cold front. Don't hide from stormy weather—the clouds can provide dramatic lighting.

Needles landscape, Chad Coppess, South Dakota Tourism

BEST PLACES TO TAKE A GROUP PORTRAIT

Say cheese!, Alan Leftridge

Record your visit to the Black Hills for posterity—take a group portrait. Most visitors look for the most memorable and iconic locations for picture backdrops. Popular spots include park entrance signs. Here are some scenic locations:

- Mount Rushmore National Memorial
- Crazy Horse Monument
- Mount Coolidge Lookout and Fire Tower
- Sylvan Lake
- Legion Lake
- Needles Eye
- Badlands National Park overlooks
- Main Street of Deadwood
- Dinosaur Park
- Devils Tower
- Roughlock Falls
- Little Spearfish Falls

You'll find plenty of fellow vacationers eager to record your memories for you.

BEST PLACES TO PEOPLE WATCH

Avenue of the Flags, NPS photo

The themes of the Black Hills are universal. The area's parks, public lands, monuments, and memorials display these themes. You came to the Black Hills for adventure, family entertainment, nature, and culture. So did everyone around you. Your experiences will be shared.

You will be among people from all over the United States and other countries. Their attire and languages may be new to you. It is entertaining to witness how others react to the wonders of the Black Hills. There are three places where scores of people gather and spend a lot of time. These are good sites to observe fellow travelers.

- Mount Rushmore National Memorial: Watch as others position themselves for a portrait with the carving as a backdrop, and stroll along the Avenue of the Flags.
- Deadwood: Main Street bustles with visitors passing in and out of shops and casinos.
- Main Street Square, Rapid City: Visitors enjoy music and an almost carnival atmosphere every summer day.

Enjoyment is infectious, particularly around crowds of people seeking the same experiences as yourself.

BEST PLACES TO SEE SUNRISE AND SUNSET

Wind Cave NP, NPS photo

While touring the Black Hills during early mornings or late afternoons, you may chance upon patterns of ever-changing colors in the eastern or western sky. Multihued sunrises and sunsets frame the landscape, provoking awe and reflection. Here are some places with great views at dawn and dusk:

- Badlands National Park
- Wildlife Loop Road
- Devils Tower National Monument
- Bear Butte
- Mount Coolidge Lookout
- Mount Roosevelt

Badlands NP, Shaina Niehans, NPS photo

EXPLORE AND DISCOVER THE NIGHT SKY!

Night sky program, Badlands NP, NPS photo

Linger after sunset and enjoy the night sky overhead. Unlike our forebears, we live with light pollution. Get in touch with what our ancestors experienced most nights of the year: the spectacular lights of the Milky Way, Venus, Jupiter, Mars, shooting stars, and the moon. Ponder what they must have seen when nights were pitch black just beyond the ring of firelight.

The Black Hills offers some of the best night sky viewing anywhere in the United States. You need to get away from the dome of light over Rapid City and other communities. The best places to see a sky full of stars are at Jewel Cave National Monument, Wind Cave National Park, Badlands National Park, Devils Tower National Monument, and Wildlife Loop Road in Custer State Park at the heart of darkness.

Get a map of the night sky from one of the visitor centers or local bookstores. Share it with your family and friends. Pick out the planets. Name the constellations and tell their stories. Night sky gazing builds memories that last a lifetime.

RESOURCES

Adams Museum
54 Sherman Street
Deadwood, SD 57732
(605) 578-1714
www.deadwoodhistory.com

Black Hills Mining Museum
323 W. Main Street
Lead, SD 57785
(605) 584-1605
bhminingmuseum@rushmore.com

Black Hills National Forest
USDA Forest Service
1019 N. 5th Street
Custer, SD 57730
(605) 673-9200
www.fs.usda.gov/blackhills

**Black Hills Visitor
Information Center**
1851 Discovery Circle
Rapid City, SD 57701
(605) 355-3700
www.blackhillsbadlands.com

Black Hills Wild Horse Sanctuary
P.O. Box 998
12165 Highland Road
Hot Springs, SD 57747
(605) 745-5955
www.wildmustangs.com

Crazy Horse Memorial
12151 Avenue of the Chiefs
Crazy Horse, SD 57730
(605) 673-4681
memorial@crazyhorse.org

**Devils Tower
National Monument**
P.O. Box 10
Devils Tower, WY 82714
(307) 467-5283 x635
www.nps.gov/deto

**Jewel Cave
National Monument**
11149 US Hwy 16, Building B12
Custer, SD 57730
(605) 673-8300
www.nps.gov/jeca

**The Journey Museum
& Learning Center**
222 New York Street
Rapid City, SD 57701
(605) 394-6923
www.journeymuseum.org

The Mammoth Site
1800 US Hwy 18 Bypass
Hot Springs, SD 57747
(605) 745-6017
www.mammothsite.com

**Mount Rushmore
National Memorial**
13000 Highway 244
Building 31, Suite 1
Keystone, SD 57751
www.nps.gov/moru

Reptile Gardens
P.O. Box 620
Rapid City, SD 57709
(605) 574-2523
www.reptilegardens.com

**Sanford Lab Homestake
Visitor Center**
160 W. Main Street
Lead, SD 57785
(605) 584-3110
www.sanfordlabhomestake.com

**South Dakota Air and
Space Museum**
2890 Davis Drive, Building #5208
Ellsworth Air Force Base, SD 57706
(605) 385-5189
www.sdairandspacemuseum.com

Sturgis Motorcycle Museum
999 Main Street
Sturgis, SD 57785
(605) 347-2001
www.sturgismuseum.com

Wind Cave National Park
26611 US Hwy 385
Hot Springs, SD 57747
(605) 745-4600
www.nps.gov/wica

ASSOCIATIONS

**Badlands Natural
History Association**
P.O. Box 47
Interior, SD 57750
(605) 433-5489
www.badlandsnha.org

**Devils Tower Natural
History Association**
15 Prairie Dog Lane
P.O. Box 37
Devils Tower, WY 82714
(307) 467-5501
sandra_mooney@partner.nps.gov
www.devilstowernha.org

Mount Rushmore Society
P.O. Box 1524
Rapid City, SD 57709
(605) 341-8883
info@mtrushmore.org
www.mountrushmoresociety.com

**Black Hills Parks &
Forests Association**
26611 US Hwy 385
Hot Springs, SD 57747
(605) 745-7020
bhpf@blackhillsparks.org
www.blackhillsparks.org

Needles Eye, Chad Coppess, South Dakota Tourism

ABOUT THE AUTHOR

Alan Leftridge is a naturalist, writer, and interpreter. He earned a biology degree at the University of Central Missouri, a secondary teaching credential from the University of Montana, and a Ph.D. in science education at Kansas State University. His enthusiasm for the outdoors led him to work as a seasonal park naturalist and a wilderness ranger. Alan was a professor of environmental education at Miami University and environmental studies at Humboldt State University. He worked as the executive editor of the Interpreter *and* Legacy *magazines for twenty years. He continues to advance the art of interpretive writing through seminars for organizations and government agencies worldwide. This is his fifth book in the* Best of *series, including* The Best of Yellowstone National Park, The Best of Glacier National Park, The Best of Rocky Mountain National Park, *and* The Best of Olympic National Park. *Alan's other books are* Glacier Day Hikes, Seeley-Swan Day Hikes, Going to Glacier, *and* Interpretive Writing. *Alan lives in the Swan Valley of northwestern Montana.*